HAZUS® MH
Estimated Annualized Earthquake Losses for the United States

FEMA 366 / April 2008

FEMA

The work that provided the basis for this publication was supported by funding from the Federal Emergency Management Agency (FEMA) under a contract with the National Institute of Building Sciences (NIBS). The substance and findings of that work are dedicated to the public. NIBS is responsible for managerial support and the services of the Earthquake Committee for reviewing drafts, and PBS&J for conducting the HAZUS-MH analyses. Individual copies or bulk rate orders of this report are available through the FEMA Distribution Center at 1-800-480-2520.

For information contact:

Eric Berman

HAZUS Program Manager

FEMA

500 C Street, SW

Washington, DC 20472

Fax: 202-646-2787

E-mail: eric.berman@dhs.gov

Website: http://www.fema.gov/plan/prevent/hazus

About the Cover

On October 17, 1989, at 5:04:15 p.m. (PDT), a magnitude 6.9 earthquake severely shook the San Francisco and Monterey Bay regions. The epicenter was located near Loma Prieta peak in the Santa Cruz Mountains, approximately 14 km (9 mi) northeast of Santa Cruz and 96 km (60 mi) south-southeast of San Francisco. Approximately 16,000 housing units were uninhabitable after the earthquake including 13,000 in the San Francisco Bay region. Another 30,000-35,000 units were moderately damaged in the earthquake.

Acknowledgments

The Federal Emergency Management Agency acknowledges and appreciates the contributions of the following individuals and organizations to the development of this report:

- Federal Emergency Management Agency — Washington, DC
  Frederick Sharrocks, Eric Berman, Edward Laatsch, and Doug Bausch

- National Institute of Building Sciences — Washington, DC
  Philip Schneider and Barbara Schauer

- PBS&J — Atlanta, Georgia
  Pushpendra Johari, Jawhar Bouabid, Sandeep Mehndiratta, R. Scott Lawson, Mourad Bonhafs, and Michelle Palmer

- Reviewers —
  Dr. Robert V. Whitman, Professor Emeritus, Massachusetts Institute of Technology, Chairman Emeritus and member of the HAZUS Earthquake Committee

  Dr. Stuart Nishenko, Consultant, San Mateo, CA

Table of Contents

Executive Summary

Recent earthquakes around the world show a pattern of steadily increasing damages and losses that are due primarily to two factors: (1) significant growth in earthquake-prone urban areas and (2) vulnerability of the older building stock, including buildings constructed within the past 20 years. In the United States, earthquake risk has grown substantially with development while the earthquake hazard has remained relatively constant. Understanding the hazard requires studying earthquake characteristics and locales in which they occur while understanding the risk requires an assessment of the potential damage to the built environment and to the welfare of people — especially in high risk areas.

Estimating the varying degree of earthquake risk throughout the United States is useful for informed decision-making on mitigation policies, priorities, strategies, and funding levels in the public and private sectors. For example, potential losses to new buildings may be reduced by applying seismic design codes and using specialized construction techniques. However, decisions to spend money on either of those solutions require evidence of risk. In the absence of a nationally accepted criterion and methodology for comparing seismic risk across regions, a consensus on optimal mitigation approaches has been difficult to reach.

While there is a good understanding of high risk areas such as Los Angeles, there is also growing recognition that other regions such as New York City and Boston have a low earthquake hazard but are still at high risk of significant damage and loss. This high risk level reflects the dense concentrations of buildings and infrastructure in these areas constructed without the benefit of modern seismic design provisions. In addition, mitigation policies and practices may not have been adopted because the earthquake risk was not clearly demonstrated and the value of using mitigation measures in reducing that risk may not have been understood.

This study highlights the impacts of both high risk and high exposure on losses caused by earthquakes. It is based on loss estimates generated by HAZUS®-MH, a geographic information system (GIS)-based earthquake loss estimation tool developed by the Federal Emergency Management Agency (FEMA) in cooperation with the National Institute of Building Sciences (NIBS). The HAZUS tool provides a method for quantifying future earthquake losses. It is national in scope, uniform in application, and comprehensive in its coverage of the built environment.

This study estimates seismic risk in all regions of the United States by using two interrelated risk indicators:

- The Annualized Earthquake Loss (AEL), which is the estimated long-term value of earthquake losses to the general building stock in any single year in a specified geographic area (e.g., state, county, metropolitan area); and

- The Annualized Earthquake Loss Ratio (AELR), which expresses estimated annualized loss as a fraction of the building inventory replacement value.

While building-related losses are a reasonable indicator of relative regional earthquake risk, it is important to recognize that these estimates are not absolute determinants of the total risk from earthquakes. This study also presents the earthquake risk in terms of amount of debris generated and social losses including casualty estimates, displaced households, and shelter requirements. Seismic risk also depends on other parameters not included herein such as damages to lifelines and other critical facilities and indirect economic loss.

The HAZUS-MH analysis indicates that the Annualized Earthquake Loss (AEL) to the national building stock is $5.3 billion per year. The majority (77 percent) of average annual loss is located on the West Coast (California, Oregon, Washington) with 66 percent ($3.5 billion per year) concentrated in the state of California. The high concentration of loss in California is consistent with the state's high seismic hazard and large structural exposure. The remaining 23 percent (1.1 billion per year) of annual loss is distributed throughout the rest of the United States (including Alaska and Hawaii) as reflected in Figure 1.

While the majority of economic loss is concentrated along the West Coast, the distribution of relative earthquake risk, as measured by the Annualized Earthquake Loss Ratio (AELR), is much broader and reinforces the fact that earthquakes are a national problem. There are relatively high earthquake loss ratios throughout the western and central United States (states within the New Madrid Seismic Zone) and in the Charleston, South Carolina area.

Forty-three metropolitan areas, led by the Los Angeles and San Francisco Bay areas, account for 82 percent of the total Annualized Earthquake Loss (AEL). Los Angeles County alone has about 25 percent of the total AEL, and the Los Angeles and San Francisco Bay areas together account for nearly 40% of the total AEL. This observation supports the need for strategies to reduce the current seismic risk by focusing on rehabilitation or replacement of the existing building stock in our most at-risk communities. Strategies to reduce future losses throughout the nation need to be closely integrated with policies and programs that guide urban planning and development.

When casualties, debris, and shelter data are aggregated by state, California accounts for nearly 50% of estimated debris generated, 60% of displaced households, and 55% of short-term shelter needs.

Loss estimates are based on the best science and engineering that was available when the study was conducted; thus, future estimates based on new technology will be different from those presented herein. To demonstrate how risk has changed with time, comparisons are drawn with FEMA 366, HAZUS®99 *Estimated Annualized Earthquake Loss for the United States*, prepared in 2001.

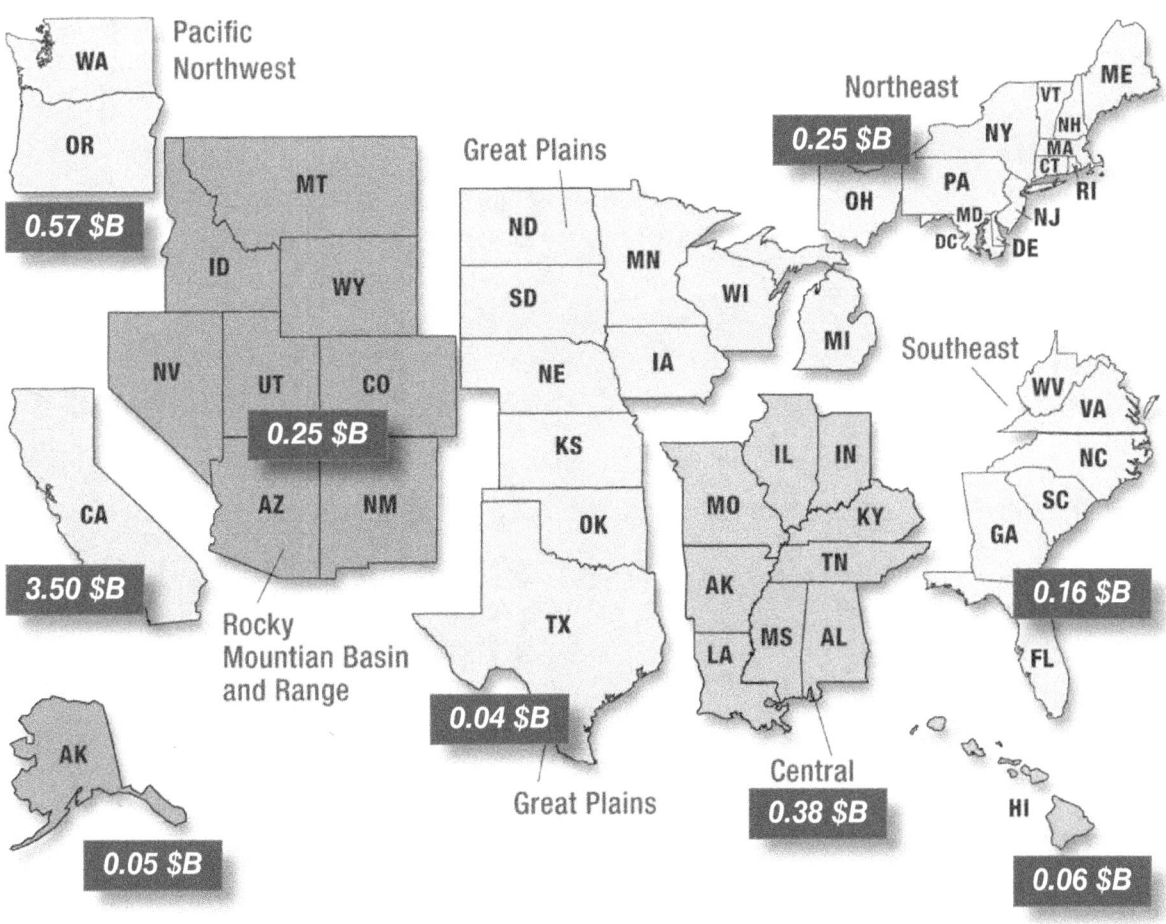

Figure E-1. Comparison of U.S. Regional Seismic Risk by Annualized Earthquake Losses (AEL).

This loss study is an important milestone in a long-term, FEMA-led effort to analyze and compare the seismic risk across regions in the United States and contributes to the mission of the National Earthquake Loss Reduction Program (NEHRP) – to develop and promote knowledge and mitigation practices and policies that reduce fatalities, injuries, and economic and other expected losses from earthquakes. The results of this study are useful in at least five ways:

- Improving our understanding of the seismic risk in the nation,

- Providing a baseline for earthquake policy development and the comparison of mitigation alternatives,

- Supporting the adoption and enforcement of seismic provisions of building codes,

- Comparing the seismic risk with that of other natural hazards, and

- Supporting pre-disaster planning for earthquake response and recovery.

1 Introduction

BACKGROUND

Much of the current perception of earthquakes in the United States has been shaped by knowledge of the earthquake hazard, which focuses on the location and type of faulting and ground failure, and the distribution of strong ground motion, or shaking. Earthquake hazard databases and maps – produced by the U.S. Geological Survey (USGS), state geological surveys and other research institutions – provide consistent and useful data.

While hazard maps contribute to understanding earthquakes, there is increasing recognition among policy makers, researchers and practitioners of the need to analyze and map the earthquake risk in the United States. As urban development continues in earthquake prone regions there is growing concern about the exposure of buildings, lifelines (e.g. utilities and transportation systems), and people to the potential effects of destructive earthquakes.

Earthquake risk analysis begins with hazard identification, but goes beyond that to investigate the potential consequences to people and property, including buildings, lifelines, and the environment. Risk analysis is useful for communities, regions, and the nation in making better decisions and setting priorities.

The ability to compare risk across states and regions is critical to the management of the National Earthquake Hazards Reduction Program (NEHRP). At the state and community level, an understanding of seismic risk is important for planning, evaluating costs and benefits associated with building codes, and other prevention measures. An understanding of earthquake risk is important to risk management for businesses and industries, as well. And, understanding the consequences of earthquakes is critical to developing emergency operations plans for catastrophes.

This study uses Hazards U.S. Multi-hazard (HAZUS-MH) Version MR2, a PC-based standardized tool that uses a uniform engineering-based approach to measure damages, casualties and economic losses from earthquakes nationwide. HAZUS® MH MR2 was released by FEMA in 2006 and incorporates updates to the building valuation data and enhanced loss estimation functions. Appendix B contains a detailed discussion of HAZUS-MH MR2.

STUDY OBJECTIVES AND SCOPE

The objective of this study is to assess levels of seismic risk in the United States using HAZUS-MH and nationwide data. The study updates *HAZUS®99 Estimated Annualized Earthquake Losses for the United States* (FEMA 366/February 2001) and incorporates the 2002 updates to the USGS National Seismic Map and Census 2000 data to estimate annualized economic losses, and debris, shelter and casualty estimates for all fifty states.

The analysis computes two inter-related metrics to characterize earthquake risk: Annualized Earthquake Loss (AEL) and the Annualized Earthquake Loss Ratio (AELR).

The AEL addresses two key components of seismic risk: the probability of ground motion occurring in a given study area and the consequences of the ground motion in terms of physical damage and economic loss. It takes into account the regional variations in risk. For example, the level of earthquake risk in the New Madrid Seismic Zone is measurably different from the risk in the Los Angeles Basin with respect to: a) the probability of damaging ground motions, and b) the consequences of the ground motions, which are largely a function of building construction type and quality, as well as ground shaking and failure during earthquakes. Consequences vary regionally, as well. For example, the earthquake hazard is higher in Los Angeles than in Memphis, but the general building stock in Los Angeles is more resistant to the effects of earthquakes.

The AEL annualizes expected losses by averaging them per year, which factors in historic patterns of frequent smaller earthquakes with infrequent but larger events to provide a balanced presentation of earthquake risk. This enables the comparison of risk between two geographic areas, such as Los Angeles and Memphis, or California and South Carolina. The AEL values are also presented on a per capita basis, to allow comparison of relative risk across regions based on population.

The AELR is the AEL as a fraction of the replacement value of the building inventory and is useful for comparing the relative risk of events. For example, $10 million in earthquake damages in Evansville, Indiana represents a greater loss than a comparable dollar loss in San Francisco, a much larger city. The annualized loss ratio allows gauging of the relationship between AEL and building replacement value. This ratio can be used as a measure of relative risk between regions and, since it is normalized by replacement value, it can be directly compared across metropolitan areas, counties, or states.

CASUALTIES, DEBRIS AND SHELTER

This study addresses three additional dimensions of earthquake risk: casualties, debris and shelter. With FEMA's emphasis on planning for catastrophic earthquakes, estimates of casualties, debris and shelter are useful metrics.

Casualties estimates are central to medical response planning and for identifying potential lifesaving measures. For example, HAZUS-MH enables measuring reduced casualties that would result from various combinations of retrofit schemes for the general building stock.

Estimates of debris on a return period basis are useful for preparing removal and disposal plans, particularly in urban areas, and for scaling mission requirements for urban search and rescue operations. The ability to compare debris estimates on a regional, state and local scale – including estimates by category such as brick, wood, reinforced concrete and steel – is valuable for planning and preparing risk reduction strategies.

Estimating shelter requirements for households and individuals are useful for measuring the effects of building codes and other mitigation measures designed to strengthen structures to reduce damage to buildings and lessen the need for post-disaster shelter. Recent disasters continue to reinforce the critical nature of shelter planning. The ability to compare shelter needs for 250-year, 500-year and 1,000-year return periods help in estimating shelter capacity and in decision-making for investment in shelter retrofits.

This report is organized into five chapters. Chapter 2 summarizes the identification of risk parameters and describes the procedures used to develop the economic loss estimates. The actual loss estimates are presented at the state, regional, county, and metropolitan level in Chapter 3 in a series of maps and tables. Chapter 4 discusses how changes in the 1996 and 2002 versions of the USGS Seismic Hazard Maps, the Census data and building inventory affect loss estimates. The report concludes with Chapter 5 and a summary of the major findings and recommendations for using results of this work. The Appendices contain a glossary of terms as well as more detailed technical information on the methodology and data.

2 Analyzing Earthquake Risk

INTRODUCTION

Earthquake risk analysis requires measuring the likely damage, casualties, and costs of earthquakes within a specified geographic area over certain periods of time. A comprehensive risk analysis assesses various levels of the hazard, as well as the consequences to structures and populations, should an event occur. Appendix A defines terminology related to risk analysis.

There are two types of risk analyses - probabilistic and scenario. This study uses a probabilistic, or statistical, hazard analysis to measure the potential effects of earthquakes of various locations, magnitudes, and frequencies. In contrast to a single, or scenario, earthquake of a specific size and location, probabilistic analyses allow for uncertainties and randomness in the occurrences of earthquakes.

To estimate average annualized loss, a number of hazard and building structural characteristics were input to the HAZUS-MH earthquake model, as described in Table 2-1.

Computing annualized earthquake loss, annualized earthquake loss ratios, and annualized casualty, debris and shelter needs was a five step process. In the first step, the USGS earthquake hazard data were processed into a format compatible with HAZUS-MH. In the second step, the building inventory in HAZUS-MH was used to estimate losses at the census tract level for specific return periods. Third, HAZUS-MH computed the AEL. Fourth, the annualized loss values were divided by building replacement values to determine the AELRs, and in the final step, annualized casualty, debris and shelter estimates were computed. Each of the five steps is described in this section, with greater detail supplied in Appendix C.

Table 2-1. Hazard and Building Parameters Used in the Study

Parameters Used in the Study	
Geotechnical Parameters	NEHRP soil type 'D' (thick alluvium).
	2002 USGS National Seismic Hazard Map ground motion parameters for eight return periods between 100 and 2,500 years (100, 250, 500, 750, 1,000, 1,500, 2,000, and 2,500 years).
	Ground motion parameters located at the census tract centroid.
	Ground-failure effects (liquefaction, landslide) were not included in the analyses due to the lack of a nationally applicable database
Building Inventory Parameters	Basis for general building inventory exposure: 2000 U.S. Census for residential buildings, 2002 Dun & Bradstreet for nonresidential' buildings, and 2005 R.S. Means for all building replacement costs.
	Building-related direct economic losses (structural and non-structural replacement costs, contents damage, business inventory losses, business interruption, and rental income losses), debris, shelter and casualties due to ground shaking were computed. All other economic losses were ignored due to the lack of a nationally applicable database.

STEP ONE:
PREPARE PROBABILISTIC HAZARD DATA

The primary source of earthquake hazard data used in this study are probabilistic hazard curves developed by the USGS. These were processed for compatibility with HAZUS. The curves specify ground motion, such as peak ground acceleration (PGA) and spectral acceleration (SA), as a function of the average annual frequency that a level of motion will be exceeded in an earthquake. Examples of the USGS probabilistic hazard curves are illustrated in Figure 2-1 that show conversely average annual frequency of exceedance as a function of PGA for single points in seven major U.S. cities.

The USGS has developed this data for the entire U.S. (see http://earthquake.usgs.gov) as part of the National Earthquake Hazards Reduction Program (NEHRP). The curves were developed for individual points in a uniform grid that covers all 50 states and Washington, DC.

A USGS map illustrating PGA for an average return period of 1,000 years is shown in Figure 2-2.

The USGS hazard curves were converted to a HAZUS-compatible database of probabilistic ground shaking values. Probabilistic hazard data for the PGA, spectral acceleration at 0.3 seconds (SA@0.3), and spectral acceleration at 1.0 second (SA@1.0) were processed for each census tract for each of the eight different return periods. Figure 2-3 compares a HAZUS-MH seismic hazard (PGA) map for the 1,000-year return period for California to the USGS map for the same return period to illustrate that the re-mapping process does not significantly affect the estimated losses where there is little exposure at risk. The analysis uses the 2002 USGS National Seismic Maps.

The USGS-computed ground motions apply to rock (B/C soil) and have been used to modify the motions so they are applicable to a soil condition that, on average, is typical for populated metropolitan areas (D soil).

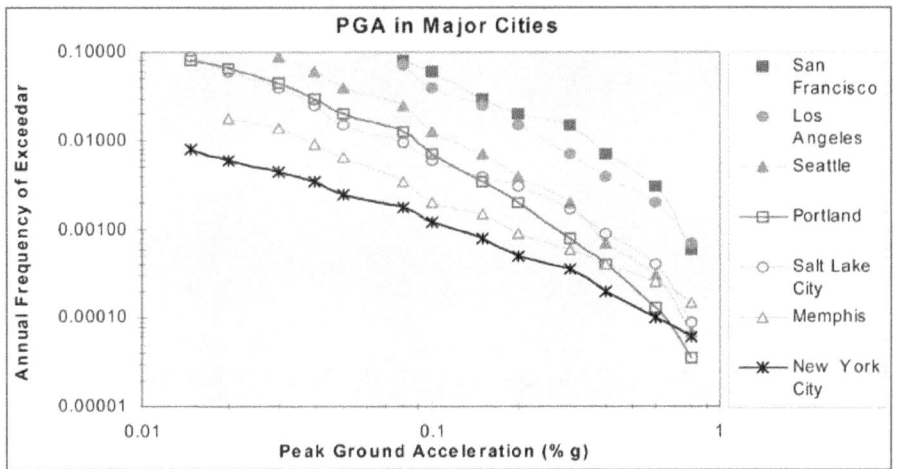

Figure 2-1.
Average Annual Frequency of Peak Ground Acceleration for Seven Major Cities

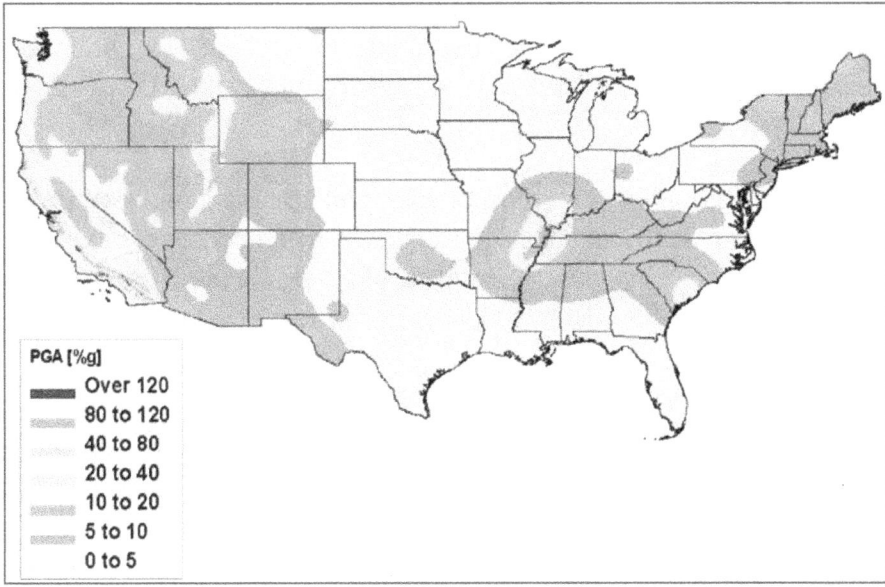

Figure 2-2.
USGS 2002 Seismic Hazard Map for the 1,000-year Return Period

Figure 2-3
Comparison of
HAZUS-MH Seismic
Hazard Map for PGA
in % g (left) and a
USGS 2002 Hazard
Map (right) for 1,000-
year Return Period
Ground Motion for a
Type B/C Soil

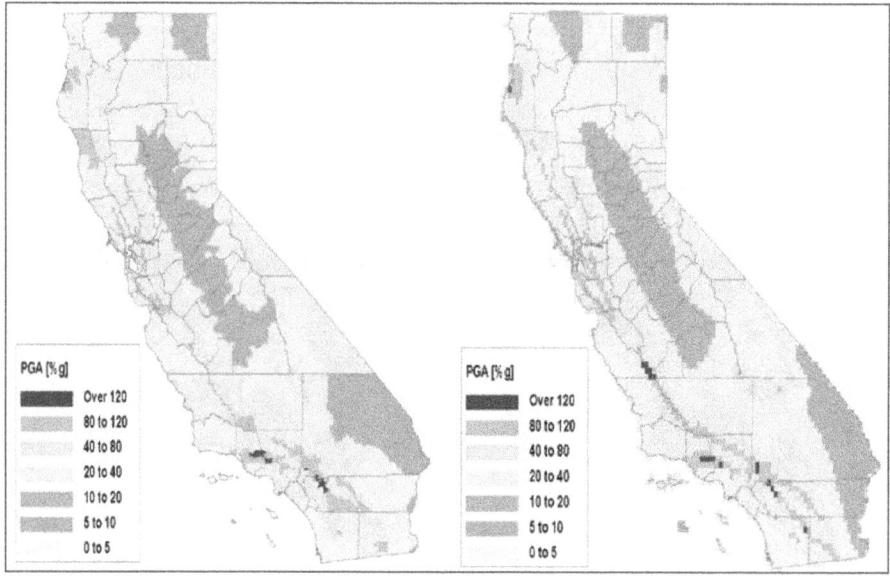

STEP TWO:
COMPUTE BUILDING DAMAGE AND LOSS

In the second step, HAZUS-MH was used to generate damage and loss estimates for the probabilistic ground motions associated with each of eight return periods. The building damage estimates were then used as the basis for computing direct economic losses. These include building repair costs, contents and business inventories losses, costs of relocation, capital-related, wage and rental losses. The analyses were completed for the entire HAZUS-MH building inventory for each of the approximately 66,000 census tracts in the U.S. These building-related losses serve as a reasonable indicator of relative regional risk, as described in greater detail in Appendix B.

Damage and economic losses to critical facilities, transportation and utility lifelines were not considered in this study. While it is understood that these losses are a component of risk, they are not included because the inventory currently available at a national scale are not comprehensive enough to yield meaningful estimates.

For the loss estimates, the replacement value of the building inventory was estimated. A map illustrating replacement value of buildings (by county) is shown in Figure 2-4. For this study, the replacement value is based only on the value of the building components and omits the land value and building contents. Building components include piping, mechanical and electrical systems, contents, fixtures, furnishings, and equipment.

The building data was combined at various levels to compare replacement value between different regions. For example, Figure 2-5 compares the replacement value by state as a percentage of total replacement value for the United States. The building exposure data help to identify concentrations of replacement value and potential areas of increased risk.

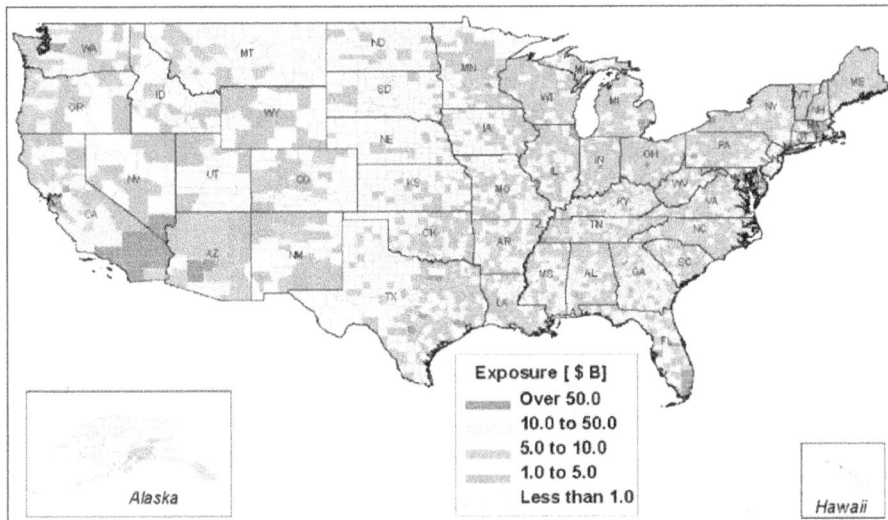

Figure 2-4
Replacement Value
of HAZUS-MH MR2
Building Inventory by
County

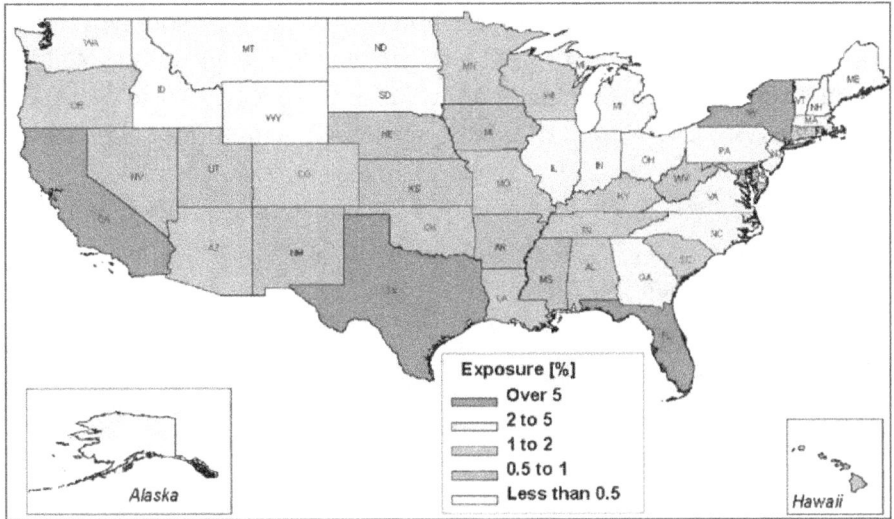

Figure 2-5
Distribution of
Building Replacement
Value by State

STEP THREE:
COMPUTE THE AVERAGE ANNUALIZED EARTHQUAKE LOSSES (AEL)

In this step, the AEL was computed by multiplying losses from eight potential ground motions by their respective annual frequencies of occurrence, and then summing the values. Several assumptions were made for this computation. First, the losses associated with ground motion with return periods greater than 2,500 years were assumed to be no worse than the losses for a 2,500-year event. Second, the losses for ground motion with less than a 100-year return period were assumed to be generally small enough to be negligible, except in California, where losses from ground motion with less than a 100-year return period can account for up to an additional 15 percent of the overall statewide AEL estimate.

STEP FOUR:
COMPUTE THE AVERAGE ANNUALIZED EARTHQUAKE LOSS RATIOS (AELR)

The AEL is an objective measure of risk, however, since risk is a function of the hazard, building stock, and vulnerability, variation in any of these three parameters affects the overall risk at any one site. Understanding how the parameters influence risk is key to developing effective risk management strategies. To facilitate that understanding for regional comparisons, the AEL was normalized by the building inventory exposure to create a loss-to-value ratio, termed the AELR, and expressed in terms of dollars per million dollars of building inventory exposure.

Between two regions with similar AEL, the region with the smaller building inventory typically has a higher relative risk, or AELR, than the region with a larger inventory, since annualized loss is expressed as a fraction of the building replacement value. For example, while Charleston, South Carolina and Memphis, Tennessee have similar AELs (see Table 3.2), the former has a higher earthquake loss ratio, since Charleston has less building inventory and building replacement value. In other words, while the seismic risk in Charleston and Memphis is roughly the same, a comparably sized earthquake would affect a significantly larger percentage of the building inventory in Charleston.

STEP FIVE:
COMPUTE THE ANNUALIZED CASUALTY, DEBRIS, AND SHELTER REQUIREMENTS

The HAZUS-MH software provides the capability to directly compute annualized casualty estimates. However, this automated capability does not exist for annualized debris and shelter estimates. To generate these estimates, HAZUS-MH was run to produce debris and shelter estimates for all eight return periods. These results then were used as inputs in a separate database utility external to HAZUS-MH to compute the annualized debris and shelter estimates. The utility used the same algorithm used by HAZUS-MH to compute the annualized economic loss and casualty estimates (described in Appendix C).

Casualties are estimated as a function of direct structural or non-structural building damage with the non-structural-related casualties derived from structural damage output. The HAZUS methodology is based on the correlation between building damage (both structural and nonstructural) and the number and severity of casualties. This method does not include casualties that might occur during or after earthquakes that are not directly related to damaged buildings such as heart attacks, car accidents, mechanical failure from power outages, incidents during post-earthquake search and rescue, post-earthquake clean-up and construction, electrocution, tsunami, landslides, liquefaction, fault rupture, dam failures, fires or hazardous materials releases. Psychological effects of earthquakes are also not modeled.

Debris is estimated using an empirical approach for two types of debris. The first is large debris, such as steel members or reinforced concrete elements of buildings, that requires special handling to break them into smaller pieces before removal. The second type of debris is smaller and more easily moved directly with bulldozers and other machinery and tools, and includes bricks, wood, glass, building contents and other materials.

Two types of shelter needs are estimated: the number of displaced households and the number of individuals requiring short-term shelter. Both are a function of the loss of habitability of residential structures directly from damage or from a loss of water and power. The methodology for calculating short-term shelter requirements recognizes that only a portion of displaced people will seek public shelter while others will seek shelter even though their residence may have no damage or insignificant damage because of reluctance to remain in a stricken area.

STUDY LIMITATIONS

The estimates provided by this study are not determinations of total risk since not all aspects of earthquakes are addressed. For example, the study only addresses direct economic losses to buildings. A comprehensive risk study would include damage to lifelines and other critical facilities, and indirect economic losses sustained by communities and regions.

There are also inherent uncertainties in computing losses using estimated building values, averaged building characteristics, spatial averaging of ground conditions, soil response and ground motion that are located at the centroids of census tracts, variables such as the magnitude and frequency of future events, and variations in the attenuation of strong ground motion. These variables must be considered when comparing the results of other loss studies based on HAZUS or other methodologies.

3 Results of the Study

In this chapter, the Annualized Earthquake Loss and the Annualized Earthquake Loss Ratios are presented at five levels of geographic resolution: nation, state, county, region, and metropolitan area.

NATION

The analysis yielded an estimate of the national AEL of $5.3 billion per year. As previously stated, this does not include losses to lifeline infrastructure or indirect (long-term) economic losses, and is therefore, a minimum estimate of the potential losses. Moreover, the estimate represents a long-term average and actual losses in any single year may be much larger or smaller.

STATES AND COUNTIES

While the AEL measures the annualized earthquake losses in any single year, the AELR addresses seismic risk in relation to the value of the buildings in the study area. By relating annualized loss to the replacement value in a given study area, the AELR provides a comparison of seismic risk between regions.

Figures 3-1 and 3-2 show the AEL and the AELR at the state level, and Figures 3-3 and 3-4 show the results at the county level. Relatively high earthquake loss ratios exist throughout the western U.S. (including Alaska and Hawaii), the central U.S. states within the New Madrid Seismic Zone, the Charleston, South Carolina area, and parts of New England, as reflected in Figures 3-2 and 3-4.

Nationwide and statewide losses are the result of averaging, over time, the losses caused by earthquakes occurring in different parts of the nation in different years. The majority (77 percent) of the annualized losses occur in California, Oregon and Washington, with 66 percent ($3.5 billion) concentrated in the state of California alone and is consistent with the State's significant building inventory and earthquake hazard (see Figures 2-2 and 2-4).

Figure 3-1
Annualized
Earthquake Losses
by State

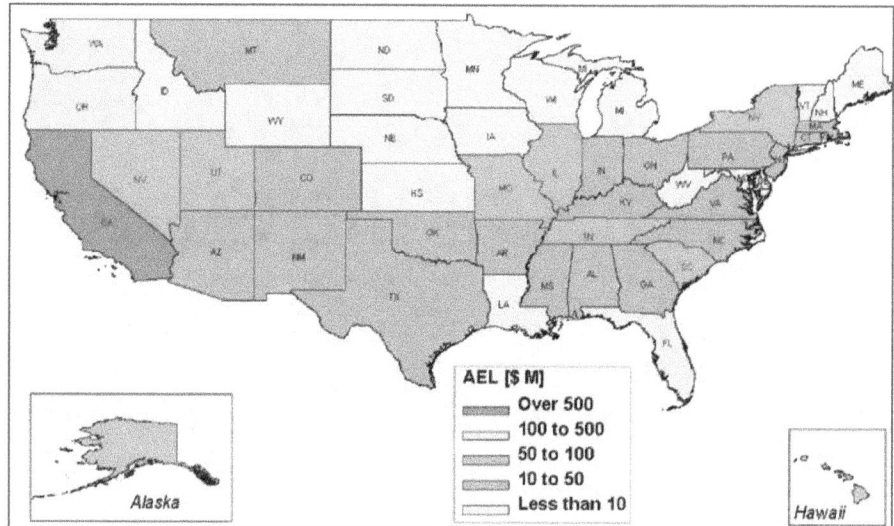

Figure 3-2
Annualized
Earthquake Loss
Ratios by State

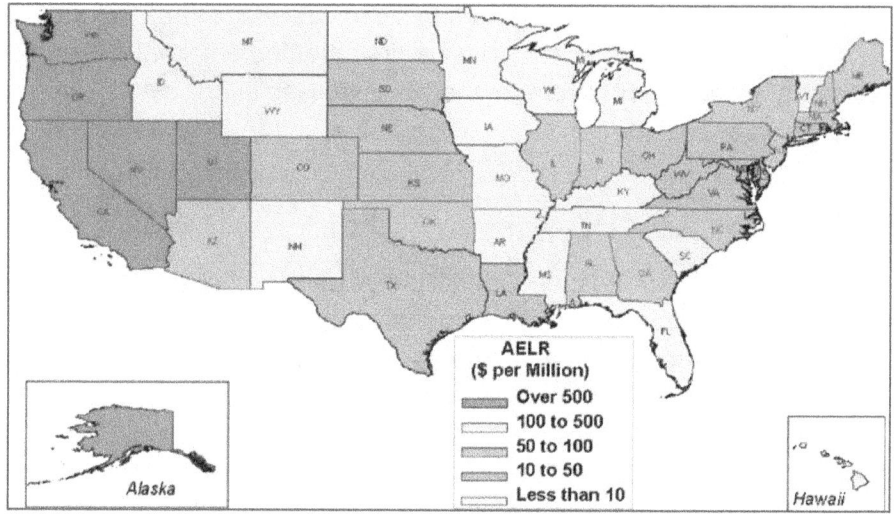

AEL and AELR values for the 50 states and Washington, D.C. are shown in Table 3-1. While California accounts for the majority of losses, the regional distribution of annualized loss and loss ratios demonstrates that seismic risk is a national concern. The juxtaposition of New York and Nevada in the AEL column of Table 3-1 illustrates the trade-offs between the value of the building inventory and the level of seismic hazard when estimating seismic risk. States with low hazard and high value building inventories (e.g., New York) can have annualized losses comparable to states with greater hazards but smaller building inventories (e.g., Nevada).

Comparing the rankings of individual states in the AEL and AELR columns of Table 3-1 shows that while California and the Pacific Northwest region retain a high relative standing, New York

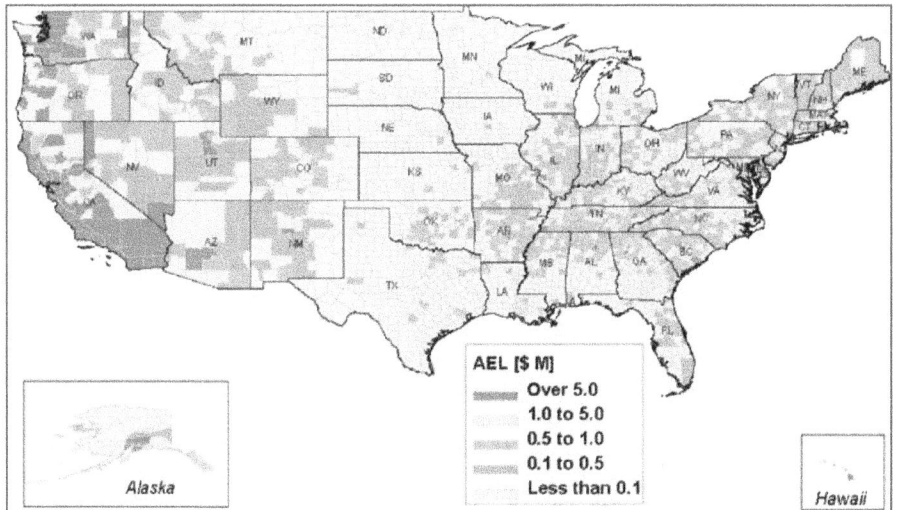

Figure 3-3
Annualized
Earthquake Losses
by County

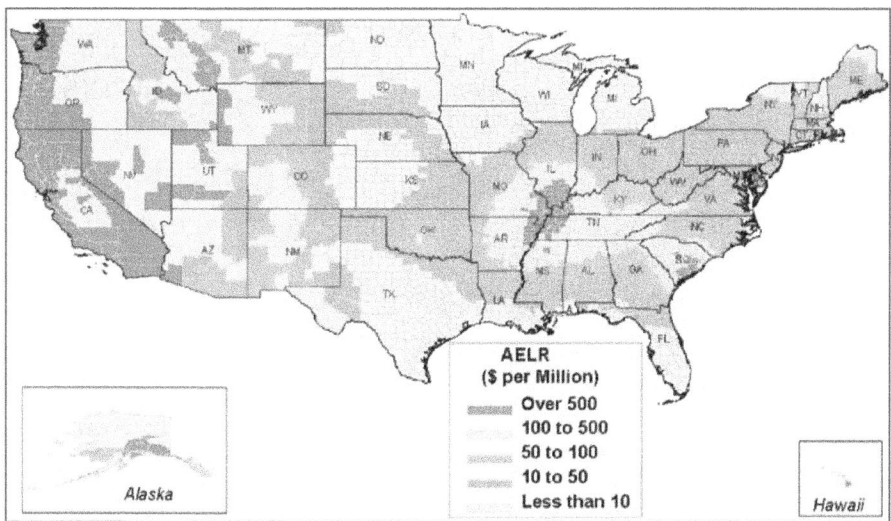

Figure 3-4
Annualized
Earthquake Losses
by County

and New Jersey, states with relatively low hazard and high inventory values, drop from 4th to 26th and 141h to 27th place, respectively. States such as Montana and New Mexico - with higher hazard and lower building inventory values - rise in the ranking from 25th to 9th and 23rd to 131h, respectively.

In other words, while the actual dollar amounts of estimated losses are lower, a significantly larger percentage of the building inventory is affected. States with the highest AELRs are located in the western United States, while other significant concentrations occur in the Southeast (South Carolina), Northeast (Vermont, New Hampshire), and the Central United States (Illinois, Kentucky, Tennessee, Arkansas, Missouri).

Table 3-1. *Ranking of States by Annualized Earthquake Loss (AEL) and Annualized Earthquake Loss Ratios (AELR)*

Rank	State	AEL ($ x 1,000)	Rank	State	AELR ($/Million $)
1	California	3,503,816	1	California	1,452
2	Washington	366,431	2	Alaska	951
3	Oregon	207,686	3	Washington	884
4	New York	95,185	4	Oregon	850
5	Tennessee	94,728	5	Utah	817
6	Utah	89,554	6	Nevada	617
7	Nevada	77,841	7	Hawaii	488
8	South Carolina	77,547	8	South Carolina	363
9	Missouri	73,082	9	Montana	304
10	Hawaii	64,961	10	Tennessee	287
11	Illinois	59,146	11	Arkansas	273
12	Alaska	52,628	12	Missouri	218
13	Arkansas	42,957	13	New Mexico	205
14	New Jersey	39,724	14	Wyoming	187
15	Kentucky	39,163	15	Kentucky	151
16	Georgia	36,733	16	Mississippi	117
17	Pennsylvania	29,585	17	Idaho	106
18	Indiana	27,999	18	Vermont	103
19	North Carolina	26,027	19	Alabama	93
20	Massachusetts	25,294	20	New Hampshire	92
21	Alabama	25,144	21	Arizona	79
22	Arizona	23,354	22	Georgia	77
23	New Mexico	20,621	23	Maine	74
24	Ohio	19,932	24	Indiana	73
25	Montana	16,725	25	Illinois	71
26	Mississippi	15,368	26	New York	67
27	Texas	14,355	27	New Jersey	63
28	Virginia	13,204	28	North Carolina	62
29	Oklahoma	11,797	29	Oklahoma	56
30	Connecticut	11,622	30	Massachusetts	51
31	Colorado	11,234	31	Connecticut	45
32	Idaho	8,042	32	Colorado	40
33	Maryland	7,218	33	Pennsylvania	37
34	New Hampshire	7,199	34	Rhode Island	36
35	Maine	5,917	35	Delaware	36
36	Florida	5,460	36	West Virginia	34
37	Wyoming	4,993	37	Virginia	32
38	Michigan	4,214	38	District of Columbia	28
39	West Virginia	4,122	39	Ohio	26
40	Vermont	3,804	40	Maryland	21
41	Louisiana	3,069	41	Kansas	14
42	Rhode Island	2,720	42	Louisiana	12
43	Kansas	2,107	43	Texas	12
44	Delaware	1,995	44	South Dakota	12
45	Wisconsin	1,613	45	Nebraska	11
46	District of Columbia	1,313	46	Michigan	6
47	Iowa	1,068	47	Iowa	6
48	Nebraska	1,021	48	Florida	6
49	Minnesota	473	49	Wisconsin	4
50	South Dakota	436	50	North Dakota	2
51	North Dakota	69	51	Minnesota	1

REGION

Figure 3-5 shows the distribution of AEL by region. Oregon, Washington, and California account for $4.0 billion in estimated annualized earthquake losses, or 77 percent of the United States total. The remaining 23 percent of estimated annualized losses are distributed across the Central United States ($0.38 billion), the Northeastern states ($0.25 billion), the Rocky Mountain/ Great Basin and Range region ($0.25 billion), the Great Plains ($0.04 billion per year), and the Southeast ($0.16 billion per year). Hawaii and Alaska have a combined AEL of $0.11 billion.

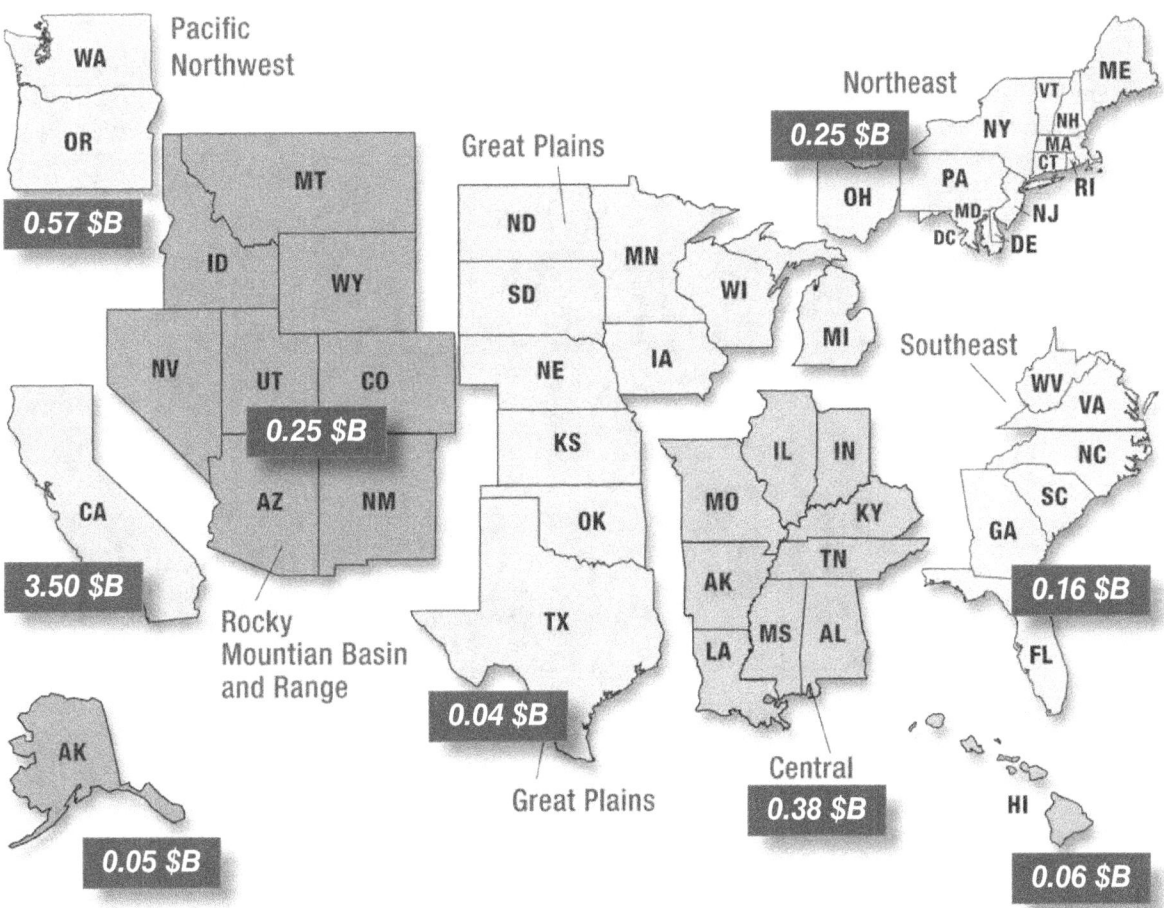

Figure 3.5 Distribution of Average Annualized Earthquake Loss by Seismic Region

METROPOLITAN AREAS

County level data in Figure 3-3 can be combined to create loss estimates for metropolitan areas, defined by the Census as the primary Metropolitan Statistical Areas (U.S. Census, 2000). Metropolitan areas with annualized losses greater than $10 million are listed in Table 3-2.

These 43 metropolitan areas, led by the Los Angeles and San Francisco Bay areas, account for 82 percent of the total annualized losses in the United States. Los Angeles alone accounts for 25 percent of the national figure. Annualized earthquake loss values for selected metropolitan areas are shown in Figures 3-6 and 3-7.

When losses for the 43 metropolitan areas are expressed as a fraction of total building value in the AELR column of Table 3-2, several cities rise in the rankings, notably Napa, CA, Anchorage, AK, and Reno, NV. Again, this is a reflection of high seismic hazard and lower relative value of building inventory.

Figure 3-6.
Metropolitan Areas
with Annualized
Earthquake Losses
Greater than $10
Million

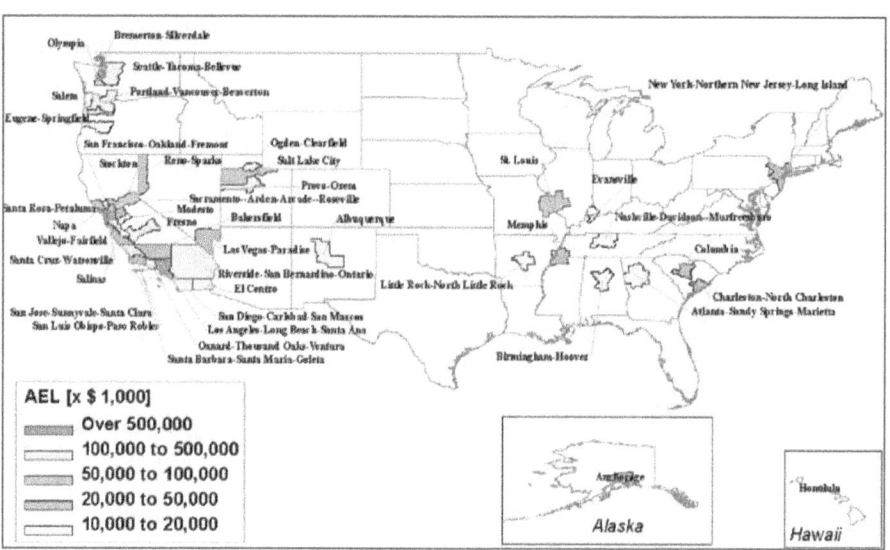

Figure 3-7.
Annualized
Earthquake
Loss Ratios for
Metropolitan Areas
with Annual Loss
Greater than $10
Million

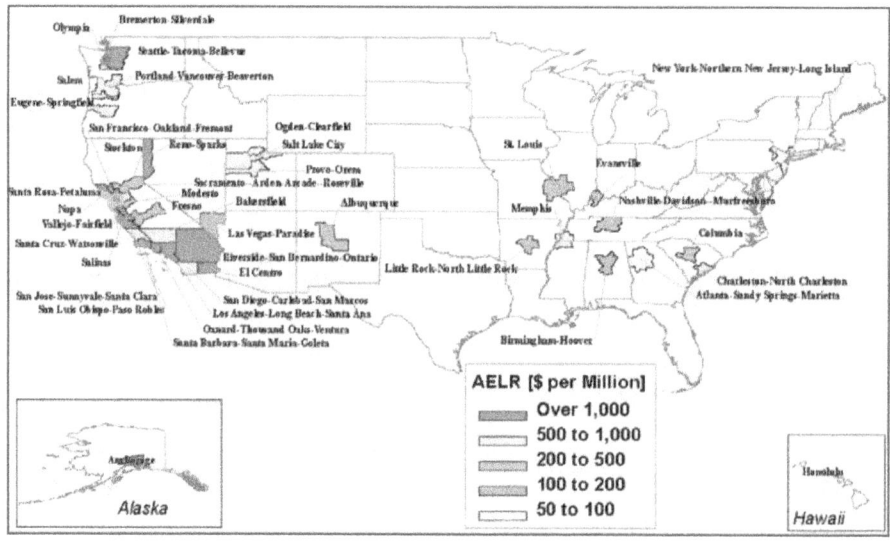

Table 3-2. Annualized Earthquake Loss (AEL) and Annualized Earthquake Loss Ratios (AELR) for 43 Metropolitan Areas with AEL Greater Than $10 Million

Rank	State	AEL ($ Million)	Rank	State	AELR ($/Million $)
1	Los Angeles-Long Beach-Santa Ana, CA	1,312.3	1	San Francisco-Oakland-Fremont, CA	2,049.44
2	San Francisco-Oakland-Fremont, CA	781.0	2	Riverside-San Bernardino-Ontario, CA	2,021.57
3	Riverside-San Bernardino-Ontario, CA	396.5	3	El Centro, CA	1,973.77
4	San Jose-Sunnyvale-Santa Clara, CA	276.7	4	Oxnard-Thousand Oaks-Ventura, CA	1,963.00
5	Seattle-Tacoma-Bellevue, WA	243.9	5	San Jose-Sunnyvale-Santa Clara, CA	1,837.58
6	San Diego-Carlsbad-San Marcos, CA	155.2	6	Santa Rosa-Petaluma, CA	1,662.57
7	Portland-Vancouver-Beaverton, OR-WA	137.1	7	Santa Cruz-Watsonville, CA	1,580.97
8	Oxnard-Thousand Oaks-Ventura, CA	111.0	8	Los Angeles-Long Beach-Santa Ana, CA	1,574.85
9	Santa Rosa-Petaluma, CA	68.6	9	Napa, CA	1,398.18
10	St. Louis, MO-IL	58.5	10	Vallejo-Fairfield, CA	1,375.94
11	Salt Lake City, UT	52.3	11	Anchorage, AK	1,238.56
12	Sacramento-Arden-Arcade--Roseville, CA	52.0	12	Santa Barbara-Santa Maria-Goleta, CA	1,207.93
13	Vallejo-Fairfield, CA	39.8	13	Reno-Sparks, NV	1,150.40
14	Memphis, TN-MS-AR	38.2	14	Bremerton-Silverdale, WA	1,110.13
15	Santa Cruz-Watsonville, CA	36.2	15	Salinas, CA	1,075.54
16	Anchorage, AK	34.8	16	Seattle-Tacoma-Bellevue, WA	1,052.43
17	Santa Barbara-Santa Maria-Goleta, CA	34.4	17	Salt Lake City, UT	984.61
18	Las Vegas-Paradise, NV	33.1	18	Olympia, WA	969.50
19	Honolulu, HI	32.0	19	Portland-Vancouver-Beaverton, OR-WA	942.62
20	Bakersfield, CA	30.3	20	Bakersfield, CA	870.43
21	New York-Northern New Jersey-Long Island, NY-NJ-PA	29.9	21	San Luis Obispo-Paso Robles, CA	848.65
22	Salinas, CA	29.2	22	Ogden-Clearfield, UT	826.52
23	Reno-Sparks, NV	29.0	23	Salem, OR	797.50
24	Charleston-North Charleston, SC	22.3	24	San Diego-Carlsbad-San Marcos, CA	770.20
25	Columbia, SC	21.6	25	Charleston-North Charleston, SC	766.01
26	Stockton, CA	20.9	26	Eugene-Springfield, OR	701.95
27	Atlanta-Sandy Springs-Marietta, GA	19.1	27	Provo-Orem, UT	683.30
28	Bremerton-Silverdale, WA	17.7	28	Stockton, CA	597.79
29	Ogden-Clearfield, UT	17.5	29	Memphis, TN-MS-AR	509.13
30	Salem, OR	17.4	30	Evansville, IN-KY	485.60
31	Eugene-Springfield, OR	16.5	31	Columbia, SC	478.05
32	Napa, CA	15.9	32	Modesto, CA	473.60
33	San Luis Obispo-Paso Robles, CA	15.7	33	Las Vegas-Paradise, NV	390.28
34	Nashville-Davidson--Murfreesboro, TN	15.4	34	Sacramento--Arden-Arcade--Roseville, CA	374.73
35	Albuquerque, NM	14.7	35	St. Louis, MO-IL	337.23
36	Olympia, WA	13.7	36	Albuquerque, NM	322.20
37	Modesto, CA	13.0	37	Honolulu, HI	311.12
38	Fresno, CA	12.6	38	Fresno, CA	283.13
39	Evansville, IN-KY	11.7	39	Little Rock-North Little Rock, AR	248.74
40	Birmingham-Hoover, AL	11.3	40	Nashville-Davidson-Murfreesboro, TN	167.26
41	El Centro, CA	10.7	41	Birmingham-Hoover, AL	115.54
42	Little Rock-North Little Rock, AR	10.5	42	Atlanta-Sandy Springs-Marietta, GA	65.39
43	Provo-Orem, UT	10.4	43	New York-Northern New Jersey-Long Island, NY-NJ-PA	20.90

SOCIO-ECONOMICS

The ability to correlate population density and annualized loss is useful for developing policies, programs and strategies to minimize socio-economic loss from earthquakes. The ability to examine annualized loss in terms of other demographic parameters such as ethnicity, age, and income is also important. Figures 3-8 and 3-9 present the AEL values on a per capita basis by county and state to show where effects on people are most pronounced. These figures also show annualized loss in relation to 2000 population distribution and reveal two important facts:

1. The high rankings include areas with high seismic hazard and high building exposure (e.g., Los Angeles and San Francisco Bay areas), but also areas with high seismic hazard and low building exposure (e.g., Hawaii and Alaska); and

2. California, Oregon, Washington, Alaska and Hawaii have the highest seismic risk when measured on a per capita basis at the state level.

Figure 3-8.
AEL Per Capita at the
County Level

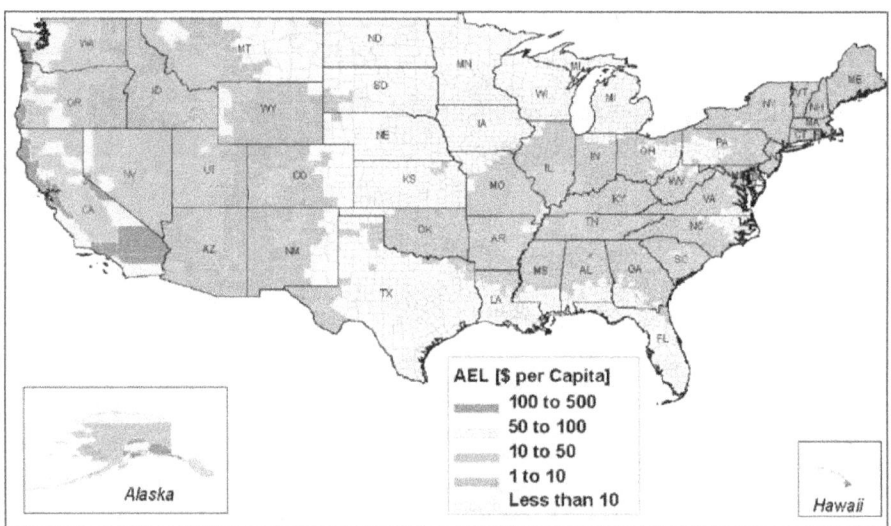

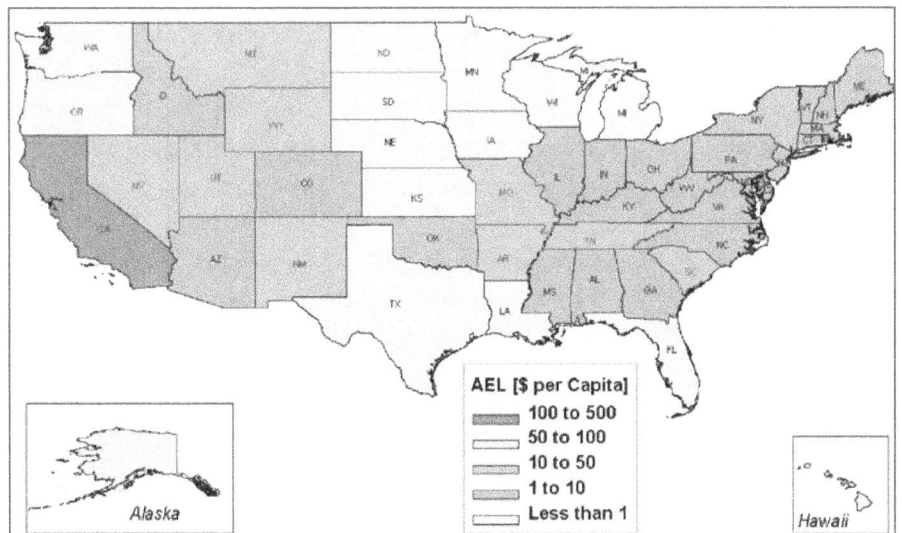

Figure 3-9.
AEL Per Capita at the
State Level

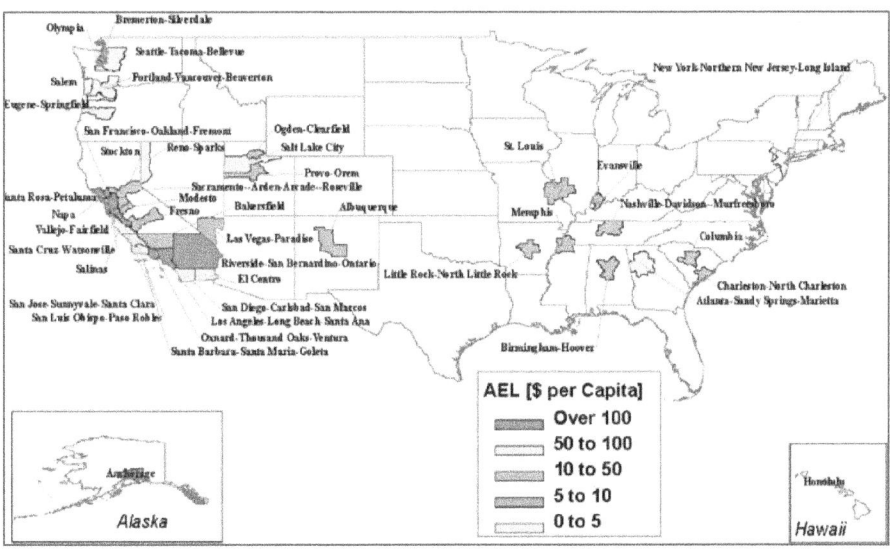

Figure 3-10.
AEL Per Capita
for Selected
Metropolitan Areas

ANNUALIZED ESTIMATES OF CASUALTIES, DEBRIS, AND SHELTER REQUIREMENTS

Estimates were made of casualties, debris, and shelter requirements for all eight return periods using HAZUS-MH. Debris and shelter requirements were then exported and used to compute annualized losses outside of HAZUS. This section highlights the findings of the analysis.

Tables 3-3 and 3-4 show the annualized estimates of debris generated and displaced households. California, Washington and Oregon together account for nearly 65 percent of estimated debris and 75 percent of displaced households. California alone accounts for nearly 50 percent of debris and 60 percent of displaced households. New York is at the top of the Eastern states contributing about 3 percent to displaced households. Tennessee ranks relatively high in debris (4th) and displaced households (5th), which can be attributed in large part to the vulnerability of the Memphis region to earthquakes in the New Madrid Seismic Zone, and the concentrations of un-reinforced masonry structures in urban areas.

Table 3-3 and Figure 3-11 and 3-12 depict the estimates of debris for 250-year and 1,000-year return periods, respectively. (Table 3-3 includes the 500-year return period). A cursory examination of the two maps shows larger increases in debris estimates for the 1,000-year return period event, notably the states in the New Madrid Seismic Zone (Tennessee, Arkansas, Missouri, Illinois, Alabama, Ohio), as well as New York, South Carolina, North Carolina and Oregon.

Figure 3-11
Estimates of Debris
Generated for 250
Year Return Period

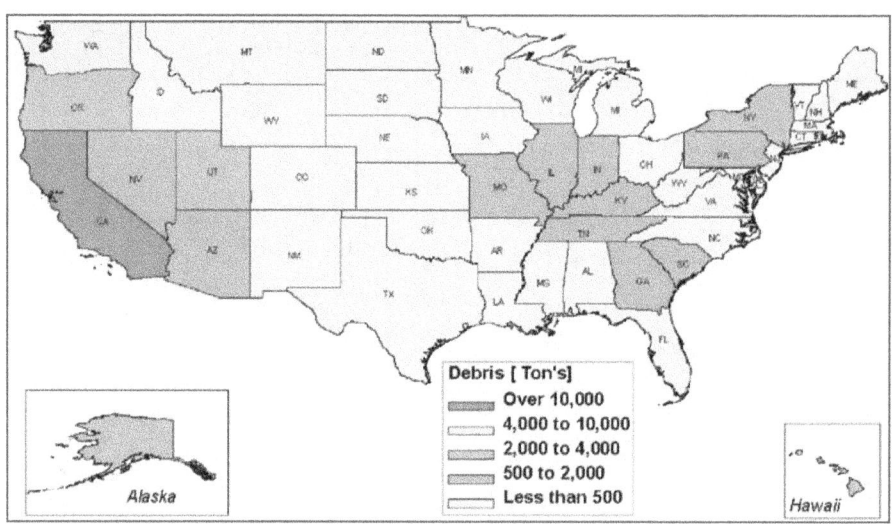

Figure 3-12
Estimates of Debris
Generated for 1000
Year Return Period

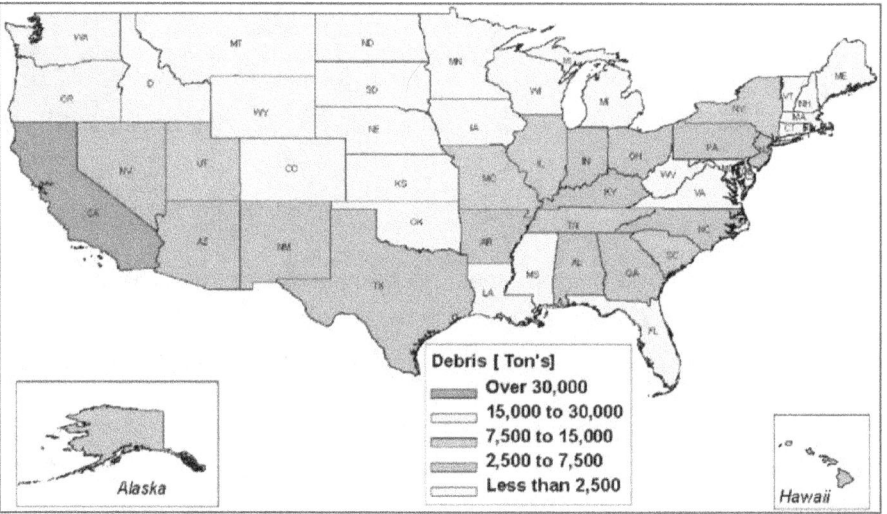

Table 3-3. Estimates of Debris (x 1000 tons)

Rank	State	Annualized Estimate	250 Year Event	500 Year Event	1000 Year Event
1	California	985	66071	136187	188556
2	Washington	130	8117	18714	26629
3	Oregon	80	3184	11436	19937
4	Tennessee	51	1169	4620	12370
5	Utah	48	2184	6982	12070
6	Missouri	43	1099	3945	10208
7	South Carolina	41	563	2726	9933
8	New York	41	966	3036	8193
9	Illinois	35	131	3458	8468
10	Nevada	31	1539	3983	6636
11	Arkansas	26	409	2233	6727
12	Kentucky	23	600	2081	5195
13	Georgia	20	95	1427	3680
14	Arizona	20	675	1649	3557
15	Hawaii	20	1198	2656	4143
16	Pennsylvania	19	605	1699	4345
17	Indiana	18	558	1638	4012
18	New Jersey	16	354	1170	3240
19	Alabama	15	260	852	2695
20	Alaska	15	1044	2348	3091
21	New Mexico	15	386	1358	3452
22	North Carolina	14	262	944	2779
23	Ohio	13	497	1317	3012
24	Texas	11	190	939	2561
25	Massachusetts	10	277	800	2116
26	Virginia	10	299	902	2204
27	Mississippi	10	150	673	2194
28	Oklahoma	9	247	765	1914
29	Montana	8	436	894	1623
30	Colorado	7	181	516	1352
31	Florida	6	1	494	1943
32	Maryland	5	176	526	1290
33	Connecticut	5	117	348	960
34	New Hampshire	3	79	220	603
35	West Virginia	3	5	289	659
36	Maine	3	71	196	526
37	Michigan	3	19	329	821
38	Wyoming	3	109	308	590
39	Louisiana	2	27	207	557
40	Idaho	2	85	229	465
41	Vermont	2	56	147	380
42	Kansas	1	41	131	317
43	Delaware	1	32	98	262
44	Rhode Island	1	31	85	233
45	District of Columbia	1	39	112	266
46	Wisconsin	1	1	101	322
47	Iowa	1	7	84	217
48	Nebraska	1	9	66	175
49	Minnesota	0	0	3	97
50	South Dakota	0	5	28	75
51	North Dakota	0	0	1	14

Table 3-4. Estimates of Displaced Households

Rank	State	Annualized Estimate	250 Year Event	500 Year Event	1000 Year Event
1	California	5130	269782	634520	1040471
2	Washington	521	29778	71224	106662
3	Oregon	313	10205	41158	76754
4	New York	204	2500	10867	35811
5	Tennessee	141	1679	9651	33253
6	Utah	166	4521	20213	40532
7	Missouri	136	1646	8809	31603
8	South Carolina	116	715	5283	27324
9	Nevada	118	4609	13586	25466
10	Illinois	98	0	7312	23738
11	Arkansas	72	434	4235	17530
12	New Jersey	65	723	3292	11067
13	Alaska	64	3886	9585	13666
14	Kentucky	49	732	3743	11932
15	Georgia	43	108	2448	7345
16	Massachusetts	46	783	2834	8568
17	Hawaii	62	3081	7934	13369
18	Pennsylvania	35	526	2024	6946
19	New Mexico	30	321	1494	5153
20	Arizona	29	576	1868	4742
21	Indiana	30	571	2087	6585
22	North Carolina	24	219	1028	3903
23	Alabama	17	216	773	2963
24	Ohio	17	122	1634	4503
25	Montana	17	696	1661	3487
26	Mississippi	15	135	733	3170
27	Virginia	16	252	1000	3080
28	Connecticut	17	19308	1009	3188
29	Texas	13	157	889	2793
30	Oklahoma	12	150	670	2142
31	Colorado	11	126	476	1663
32	New Hampshire	11	179	573	1741
33	Maine	8	148	456	1327
34	Maryland	8	147	586	1841
35	Florida	6	0	302	1547
36	Vermont	6	120	351	1010
37	Rhode Island	5	89	302	955
38	Wyoming	5	124	453	1039
39	West Virginia	4	2	250	715
40	Michigan	4	17	347	1056
41	Idaho	4	76	261	694
42	Louisiana	2	21	203	682
43	District of Columbia	2	42	163	493
44	Wisconsin	2	1	159	586
45	Delaware	2	25	98	353
46	Kansas	2	39	145	439
47	Iowa	1	8	85	264
48	Nebraska	1	8	69	238
49	South Dakota	0	5	34	113
50	Minnesota	0	0	2	115
51	North Dakota	0	0	1	18

Tables 3-5 and 3-6 show the annualized estimates of the number of people looking for shelter (shelter requirement) and the annualized estimates of number of people looking for shelter per million of population for all the states. The estimates of shelter requirements follow the trend of displaced households with California, Washington and Oregon together accounting for nearly 75 percent, and California accounting for nearly 60 percent of the total. New York remains the top contributor from the Eastern states with about 3 percent of total number of people looking for shelter.

A comparison of the standings of individual states in the Shelter and Shelter Ratio columns of Tables 3-5 and 3-6 show that while California, Oregon and Washington rank in the top tier, New York and New Jersey – states with relatively low hazard and high population – drop from 4th to 15th and 121h to 20th place, respectively. Alaska and Hawaii - with higher hazard and lower population – rise in the ordering from 13th to 3rd and 17th to 71h, respectively.

Figures 3-13 and 3-14 depict the estimates of shelter requirements generated for a 250-year and 1,000-year return period, respectively, aggregated at state level. Table 3-5 includes the annualized and 250-, 500-, and 1,000-year return period estimates.

Table 3-5. Estimates of Short –Term Shelter Requirements (# of People)

Rank	State	Annualized Estimate	250 Year Event	500 Year Event	1000 Year Event
1	California	1313	70093	163635	265335
2	Washington	123	7036	16870	25276
3	Oregon	77	2532	10263	19110
4	New York	58	703	3070	10118
5	Tennessee	40	479	2788	9556
6	Utah	39	1096	4850	9596
7	Missouri	36	445	2413	8587
8	South Carolina	32	201	1478	7604
9	Nevada	30	1201	3539	6620
10	Illinois	25	0	1954	6273
11	Arkansas	21	124	1224	5033
12	New Jersey	17	187	853	2861
13	Alaska	14	842	2066	2939
14	Kentucky	14	205	1039	3272
15	Georgia	12	29	670	2024
16	Massachusetts	12	197	713	2151
17	Hawaii	11	551	1431	2436
18	Pennsylvania	9	137	526	1800
19	New Mexico	8	91	424	1445
20	Arizona	8	162	526	1318
21	Indiana	8	148	536	1679
22	North Carolina	6	59	276	1051
23	Alabama	5	64	229	873
24	Ohio	5	0	431	1184
25	Montana	4	185	441	924
26	Mississippi	4	41	215	920
27	Connecticut	4	4991	262	827
28	Virginia	4	65	260	798
29	Texas	4	51	263	814
30	Oklahoma	3	40	178	565
31	Colorado	3	31	118	410
32	New Hampshire	2	42	135	409
33	Maine	2	39	120	350
34	Maryland	2	38	149	465
35	Florida	2	0	80	405
36	Vermont	1	30	87	249
37	Rhode Island	1	24	82	260
38	Wyoming	1	27	100	231
39	West Virginia	1	1	72	206
40	Michigan	1	4	91	275
41	Idaho	1	19	65	172
42	Louisiana	1	7	62	209
43	District of Columbia	1	12	48	146
44	Wisconsin	0	0	40	149
45	Delaware	0	6	24	87
46	Kansas	0	10	37	111
47	Iowa	0	2	22	66
48	Nebraska	0	2	17	60
49	South Dakota	0	1	9	28
50	Minnesota	0	0	0	28
51	North Dakota	0	0	0	5

Table 3-6. Annualized Shelter Requirement Ratios

Rank	State	Shelter Ratio (# of People/Million)
1	California	39
2	Oregon	23
3	Alaska	22
4	Washington	21
5	Utah	18
6	Nevada	15
7	Hawaii	9
8	South Carolina	8
9	Arkansas	8
10	Tennessee	7
11	Missouri	6
12	Montana	5
13	New Mexico	5
14	Kentucky	3
15	New York	3
16	Vermont	2
17	Wyoming	2
18	Illinois	2
19	New Hampshire	2
20	New Jersey	2
21	Massachusetts	2
22	Maine	2
23	Arizona	2
24	Mississippi	2
25	Georgia	1
26	Rhode Island	1
27	Connecticut	1
28	Indiana	1
29	Alabama	1
30	District of Columbia	1
31	Oklahoma	1
32	North Carolina	1
33	Pennsylvania	1
34	Idaho	1
35	Colorado	1
36	Virginia	1
37	Delaware	1
38	West Virginia	1
39	Ohio	0
40	Maryland	0
41	Texas	0
42	Louisiana	0
43	Kansas	0
44	South Dakota	0
45	Nebraska	0
46	Florida	0
47	Michigan	0
48	Wisconsin	0
49	Iowa	0
50	North Dakota	0
51	Minnesota	0

Figure 3-11
Estimates of Debris
Generated for 250
Year Return Period

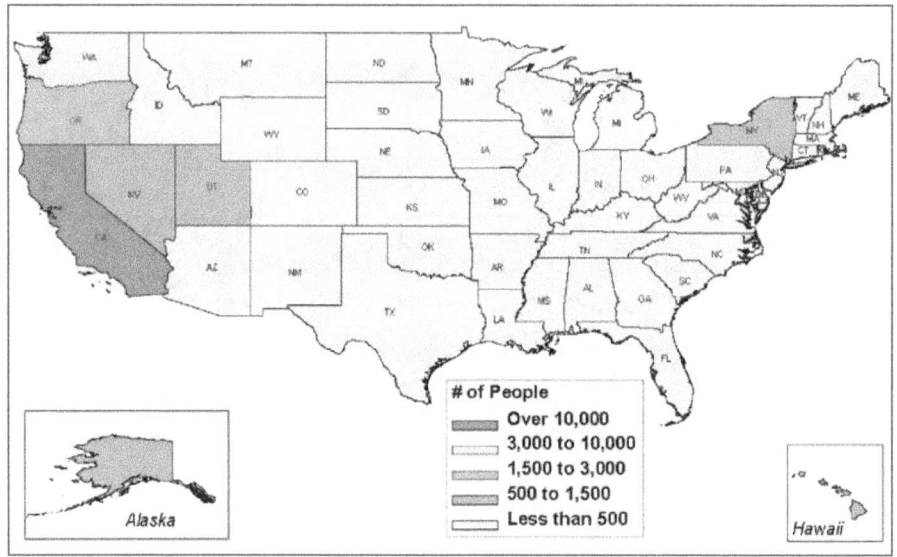

Figure 3-12
Estimates of Debris
Generated for 1000
Year Return Period

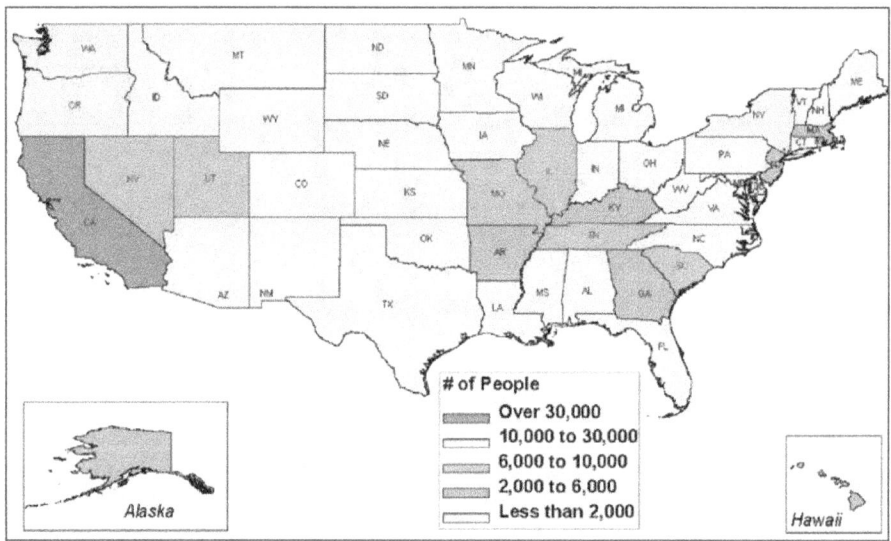

Table 3.7 divides annualized casualty estimates into three categories of injury: 1) Minor (non life-threatening); 2) Major (defined as injuries that pose an immediate life-threatening condition if not treated adequately; and 3) Fatal. Casualty rates are a direct function of the time-of-day or night that an earthquake occurs, as reflected in Table 3.7. A majority of injuries are in the minor category.

Table 3-7. Annualized Estimates of Casualties by State

Rank	State	Day Time			Night Time		
		Minor	Life Threatening	Fatal	Minor	Life Threatening	Fatal
1	California	1891	63	122	1276	19	36
2	Washington	260	9	17	127	2	4
3	Oregon	188	7	13	85	2	3
4	Utah	86	3	6	59	2	3
5	Tennessee	89	3	5	62	1	3
6	South Carolina	64	2	4	51	1	2
7	Missouri	67	2	4	62	2	3
8	Nevada	59	2	4	33	1	1
9	Illinois	45	1	2	48	1	2
10	Arkansas	38	1	2	33	1	2
11	Alaska	28	1	2	17	0	1
12	New York	45	1	2	45	1	2
13	Kentucky	31	1	2	25	1	1
14	Georgia	32	1	1	17	0	1
15	Hawaii	21	1	1	17	0	1
16	New Mexico	15	0	1	13	0	1
17	Indiana	19	0	1	17	0	1
18	Mississippi	16	0	1	11	0	0
19	New Jersey	20	0	1	16	0	1
20	Montana	12	0	1	7	0	0
21	Alabama	14	0	1	9	0	0
22	Arizona	14	0	1	15	0	0
23	North Carolina	15	0	1	11	0	0
24	Massachusetts	13	0	0	9	0	0
25	Pennsylvania	14	0	0	18	0	1
26	Texas	10	0	0	7	0	0
27	Ohio	12	0	0	10	0	0
28	Virginia	9	0	0	9	0	0
29	Oklahoma	7	0	0	8	0	0
30	Wyoming	4	0	0	2	0	0
31	New Hampshire	5	0	0	3	0	0
32	Connecticut	6	0	0	4	0	0
33	Colorado	6	0	0	4	0	0
34	Maine	4	0	0	2	0	0
35	Idaho	3	0	0	2	0	0
36	Vermont	3	0	0	2	0	0
37	Maryland	4	0	0	4	0	0
38	West Virginia	3	0	0	3	0	0
39	Florida	3	0	0	5	0	0
40	Louisiana	2	0	0	2	0	0
41	Michigan	2	0	0	2	0	0
42	Rhode Island	1	0	0	1	0	0
43	Delaware	1	0	0	1	0	0
44	Kansas	1	0	0	1	0	0
45	District of Columbia	1	0	0	1	0	0
46	Wisconsin	1	0	0	1	0	0
47	Iowa	1	0	0	0	0	0
48	Nebraska	1	0	0	0	0	0
49	South Dakota	0	0	0	0	0	0
50	Minnesota	0	0	0	0	0	0
51	North Dakota	0	0	0	0	0	0

COMPARISON TO PREVIOUS STUDY

4 Comparison to Previous Study

This chapter compares the results of this study with the original earthquake loss study (FEMA 366, 2001) and analyzes how changes in the earthquake hazard and building inventory have affected potential earthquake losses. The previous study was based on methods and data in HAZUS99 which included the 1996 USGS National Seismic Hazard Maps and Census 1990 data. The current study utilizes HAZUS-MH MR2 methods and data and includes the 2002 USGS seismic maps and Census 2000 data. Two different analyses were performed, as described below.

For the Nation:

HAZUS-MH MR2 methods and data/2002 USGS National Seismic Maps. This analysis provided a snapshot of the current earthquake risk using the most up-to-date version of HAZUS and recent building, population, and hazard maps.

HAZUS-MH MR2 methods and data/1996 USGS National Seismic Hazard Maps. This analysis used the most up-to-date version of HAZUS and recent building and population data with the 1996 seismic maps used for FEMA 366 and enabled comparison of the change in earthquake risk in the past decade.

For California only:

HAZUS-MH MR2 with HAZUS99. This analysis was conducted to test the effect of the change in exposure between HAZUS-MH MR2 and HAZUS99.

STUDY PARAMETERS

In 1996, the USGS prepared a series of seismic hazard maps for earthquakes that were used in HAZUS99 for hazard characterization. The original earthquake loss study (FEMA 366, 2001) used the HAZUS99 methodology, the 1994 building data, and population data from the 1990 census. With the release of HAZUS-MH several parameters changed, as reflected in Table 4-1. Since HAZUS-MH was used as the basis for the current study, these changes are reflected in the results.

Table 4-1. Summary of Key Changes Incorporated into HAZUS-MH

HAZUS 99	HAZUS-MH
1996 National Seismic Hazard Maps	2002 USGS National Seismic Hazard Maps
Loss estimates based on 1990 Census Data	Loss estimates based on 2000 Census Data
1994 Building Inventory and Occupancy to Building Type Distributions	2002 Building Inventory (Dun and Bradstreet) and updated Occupancy to Building Type Distributions
Building and Content Exposure based on square footage from pre-defined regions	Building and Content Exposure based on General Building Stock datasets in the study region.

COMPARISON OF AEL AND AELR

The current study estimates a national AEL of $5.3 billion (2005 dollars), which is a 21% increase over the FEMA 366 estimate of $4.4 billion (1994 dollars). However, if we adjust the FEMA 366 study results to reflect current values (2005 dollars[1]), the FEMA 366 loss estimate would increase to $5.6 billion, which represents a small decrease in the overall earthquake loss potential. During the period the national building inventory increased by almost 50%, the estimated earthquake loss increased by only 20%.

In the following sections, the reasons why the loss did not increase at the same proportional rate as the building inventory will be discussed.

EFFECT OF A CHANGE IN HAZARD

To improve our understanding of how a change in a hazard (while keeping the other analysis parameters constant) affects losses, HAZUS-MH was run using the 1996 USGS Probabilistic Hazard Data and compared to results using the 2002 USGS Probabilistic Maps (which are incorporated in HAZUS-MH).

Figure 4-1 depicts the differences in hazard where the negative values represent a decrease since 1996 and the positive values represent an increase since 1996. The following patterns are noted:

- A slight decrease in the hazard in Western United States, except for some parts of Washington and Utah.

- A slight increase in the hazard in the Great Plains.

---

1 This adjustment factor is based on the average of the ENR adjustment factor (Engineering News-Record, Construction Cost History — http://www.enr.com/) and the CPI adjustment factor (Bureau of Labor Statistics, Consumer Price Index - All Urban Consumers— http://usda.mannlib.cornell.edu/reports/nassr/price/zap-bb/) as calculated with the Engineering News Record Damage Inflation Calculator: Version 2.1, July 20, 2007.

■ Little change in hazard in the Southeast, except for modest changes in some areas of Virginia, North Carolina and South Carolina and a significant increase in the Charleston area.

■ Significant increase in hazard in the Central region, which includes the New Madrid Seismic Zone.

■ Little change in hazard in the Northeast, except for some areas of New York, Maine where the hazard has gone down.

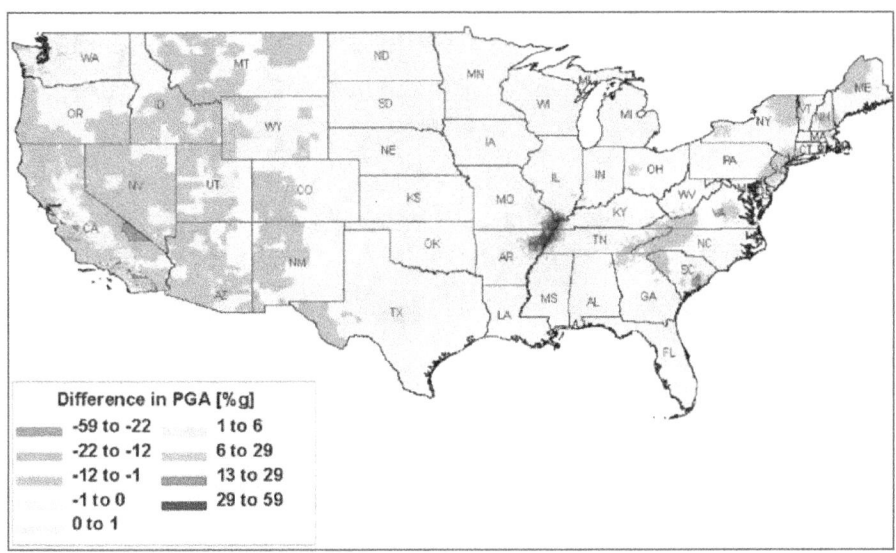

Figure 4-1
Difference in the
1,000-year return
period USGS Seismic
Hazard Map 2002
and USGS Seismic
Hazard Map 1996
(differences show
PGA 2002 values vs.
PGA 1996 values)

Table 4-2 shows the Annualized Loss obtained from HAZUS-MH MR2 using both 2002 and 1996 USGS National Seismic Hazard Maps for all the states, including the percentage change. The values in parentheses represent a decrease in losses. Analysis of the results reveals a general decrease in AEL, with some exceptions. Washington and Utah show a sight increase in losses. California shows a decrease from 74 percent of U.S. total in FEMA 366 to 66 percent of the U.S. total in this study. States in the New Madrid Seismic Zone in the Central U.S. experience an increase in AEL when using the 2002 hazard maps.

Table 4-3 lists the Annualized Loss Ratio from both the hazards for all the states. The loss ratios follow the trend of the change in loss.

For Tables 4-2 and 4-3 building inventory loss estimates were calculated by census tract and reported in 2005 dollars.

Table 4-2. National Comparison of the AEL Values in $ by State for 2002 and 1996 USGS Hazard Maps

Rank	State	AEL 2002 Hazard (x 1000)	AEL 1996 Hazard (x 1000)	Percent Change
1	California	3,503,816	3,813,745	(8)
2	Washington	366,431	336,102	9
3	Oregon	207,686	228,251	(9)
4	New York	95,185	146,906	(35)
5	Tennessee	94,728	88,374	7
6	Utah	89,554	87,948	2
7	Nevada	77,841	79,061	(2)
8	South Carolina	77,547	88,965	(13)
9	Missouri	73,082	63,669	15
10	Hawaii	64,961	70,655	(8)
11	Illinois	59,146	56,384	5
12	Alaska	52,628	55,637	(5)
13	Arkansas	42,957	33,172	29
14	New Jersey	39,724	61,218	(35)
15	Kentucky	39,163	36,417	8
16	Georgia	36,733	48,295	(24)
17	Pennsylvania	29,585	43,160	(31)
18	Indiana	27,999	26,833	4
19	North Carolina	26,027	33,767	(23)
20	Massachusetts	25,294	37,217	(32)
21	Alabama	25,144	27,531	(9)
22	Arizona	23,354	31,776	(27)
23	New Mexico	20,621	24,674	(16)
24	Ohio	19,932	22,308	(11)
25	Montana	16,725	18,847	(11)
26	Mississippi	15,368	12,852	20
27	Texas	14,355	15,072	(5)
28	Virginia	13,204	19,421	(32)
29	Oklahoma	11,797	11,115	6
30	Connecticut	11,622	18,153	(36)
31	Colorado	11,234	11,234	0
32	Idaho	8,042	8,830	(9)
33	Maryland	7,218	10,170	(29)
34	New Hampshire	7,199	10,042	(28)
35	Maine	5,917	8,046	(26)
36	Florida	5,460	6,280	(13)
37	Wyoming	4,993	5,710	(13)
38	Michigan	4,214	3,883	9
39	West Virginia	4,122	5,427	(24)
40	Vermont	3,804	5,468	(30)
41	Louisiana	3,069	3,431	(11)
42	Rhode Island	2,720	3,967	(31)
43	Kansas	2,107	1,656	27
44	Delaware	1,995	3,105	(36)
45	Wisconsin	1,613	1,628	(1)
46	District of Columbia	1,313	1,824	(28)
47	Iowa	1,068	771	39
48	Nebraska	1,021	870	17
49	Minnesota	473	362	31
50	South Dakota	436	372	17
51	North Dakota	69	57	21
	TOTAL	**5,280,295**	**5,730,658**	(9)

Table 4-3. National Comparison of the AELR Values by State for 2002 and 1996 USGS Hazard Maps

Rank	State	AELR 2002 Hazard ($ / Million)	AELR 1996 Hazard ($ / Million)
1	California	1,452	1,580
2	Alaska	951	1,005
3	Washington	884	811
4	Oregon	850	935
5	Utah	817	802
6	Nevada	617	626
7	Hawaii	488	531
8	South Carolina	363	417
9	Montana	304	332
10	Tennessee	287	268
11	Arkansas	273	210
12	Missouri	218	190
13	New Mexico	205	245
14	Wyoming	187	214
15	Kentucky	151	140
16	Mississippi	117	98
17	Idaho	106	116
18	Vermont	103	149
19	Alabama	93	102
20	New Hampshire	92	128
21	Arizona	79	108
22	Georgia	77	102
23	Maine	74	101
24	Indiana	73	70
25	Illinois	71	67
26	New York	67	104
27	New Jersey	63	97
28	North Carolina	62	80
29	Oklahoma	56	53
30	Massachusetts	51	76
31	Connecticut	45	71
32	Colorado	40	40
33	Pennsylvania	37	53
34	Rhode Island	36	53
35	Delaware	36	56
36	West Virginia	34	45
37	Virginia	32	47
38	District of Columbia	28	38
39	Ohio	26	30
40	Maryland	21	30
41	Kansas	14	11
42	Louisiana	12	14
43	Texas	12	12
44	South Dakota	12	10
45	Nebraska	11	9
46	Michigan	6	6
47	Iowa	6	4
48	Florida	6	6
49	Wisconsin	4	4
50	North Dakota	2	2
51	Minnesota	1	1

EFFECT OF CHANGE IN BUILDING INVENTORY

In HAZUS-MH, the building distribution for the inventory of California was changed significantly. The primary change in the building distribution (See Table 4-4) was a proportional in-crease in wood frame buildings (+17%) and a reduction in the amount of masonry, steel, concrete buildings. This substantial revision in the building distribution was limited to California with the distribution in other states remaining basically the same.

Generally, wood frame construction is less vulnerable to earthquake damage than other building types, so this change in inventory composition was expected to cause a reduction in the AELR for California. Consequently, since California accounted for over 2/3rds of the total AEL for the US, this change was expected to have a substantial impact on the overall study.

This reduction in normalized loss was driven primarily by the change in the building distribution but was also affected by a reduction in the USGS probabilistic seismic hazard. Additional analysis showed that 78% of the loss reduction could be attributed to the change in building distribution while 22% was due to a reduction in the probabilistic seismic hazard for California.

Table 4-4. Change in Building Distribution by General Structural Types in California

	Wood	Steel	Concrete	Masonry	Manufactured Homes
HAZUS 99	63	10	11	13	3
HAZUS-MH MR2	80	4.2	8	7	0.8
Percent Change	17.00	(5.80)	(3.00)	(6.00)	(2.20)

5 Interpretation and Applications

While there is a well-established body of information on how the earthquake hazard varies among regions, there is less understanding of how earthquake risk differs from one region to another, and how the risk may be affected by changes in the hazard itself and building inventory. From a public policy and emergency management standpoint, understanding and documenting how these changes affect regional, state and local earthquake exposure and risk are fundamental to garnering and sustaining support for risk reduction strategies, seismic policy and program development.

Study Findings

- ■ Although greatest on the West Coast, seismic risk exists in other areas of the U.S.

  The annualized loss from earthquakes nationwide is estimated to be $5.3 billion per year with California, Oregon and Washington accounting for $4.1 billion, or 77 percent. The remaining 23 percent of losses are distributed among the Central states ($0.38 billion per year), the Northeast ($0.25 billion per year), and the Southeast ($0.16 billion per year). Hawaii and Alaska have a combined $110 million in average annualized losses.

- ■ An increase in building inventory will not always translate to a proportional increase in seismic risk.

  In HAZUS-MH, the occupancy-to-building type profile for California was modified to include a higher proportion of wood frame construction (See Table 4-4). Wood frame construction is less vulnerable to earthquake damage than other types of building construction types, such as masonry construction. This modification to the building type profile was the primary reason for the reduction in the AELR for California [1,452 (HAZUS-MH) vs. 2,048 (HAZUS-99)] and is a good example of the potential loss reduction that can occur by replacing aging construction with more earthquake resistant construction.

- Earthquake risk continues to be highest in urban areas, most notably California and on the West Coast.

In a number of states - New York, South Carolina, Utah, Alaska, Hawaii, California, Oregon, and Washington - estimated losses in metropolitan areas account for up to 80 percent of total state losses, which has important implications for a national strategy to reduce seismic risk. More than 60 percent of the annualized losses in California are expected in the three metropolitan areas of San Francisco, Los Angeles and San Diego. These three metropolitan regions have a combined population of 15 million (2004) and account for over 43 percent of the total estimated annualized earthquake loss in the United States.

- An increase in the USGS probabilistic seismic maps will translate to increases in risk.

In HAZUS-MH, the probabilistic seismic hazard increased for many states in the Central US. This increase was due to changes in the USGS seismic hazard models (USGS, 2002) for the Central US and resulted in an increase in the AELR for many states. In some states, such as Arkansas, the increase in AELR was as much as 30 % (See Table 4-3).

Applications

The findings in this study can be used to support analysis, decision making and risk reduction, including:

1. To improve understanding of the seismic risk in the U.S.

This study builds on the knowledge gained from the original study (FEMA 366, 2001) to incorporate new data that directly influences earthquake loss and mitigation: 1) the seismic hazard (2002 hazard data); 2) inventory (2002 Dun and Bradstreet); 3) population at risk (2000 Census Data); and 4) estimated social losses. By modifying these important parameters, the study provides a clearer picture of their role in shaping seismic risk in the U.S. In a broader sense, the information in this study is an integral component of a "national seismic risk baseline" – aggregated at the metropolitan, county, state and regional level. Key parameters that can be updated include: 1) Seismic hazard; 2) Inventory (general building stock, lifelines, essential facilities); 3) Demographic data; and 4) Loss estimation and other analyses.

2. To support the adoption and enforcement of seismic building code provisions.

One of the objectives of the National Earthquake Hazards Reduction Program (NEHRP) is to promote the adoption and enforcement[2] of seismic building codes in regions of the U.S. that experience infrequent but damaging earthquakes. The uneven distribution of seismic risk across the U.S. militates against uniform adoption and enforcement. Typically, localities with infrequent earthquakes place a low priority on seismic code enforcement. However, this study demonstrates the actual regional risk in terms of potential damage and economic loss.

The HAZUS-MH data can be applied to evaluate the effectiveness of different mitigation strategies by measuring risk and their uncertainties before and after they are implemented. For example, a FEMA study[3] concludes that if the Los Angeles area had been built to high seismic design standards (UBC zone 4 or NEHRP zone 7) prior to the 1994 Northridge earthquake, the losses would have been reduced by $11.3 billion (including buildings, contents, and income).

This is equivalent to avoiding about 40 percent of losses (when adjusting for additional costs to design and construct to higher seismic standards). This information type of analysis is valuable when determining policy and program options in for long-term risk management measures, including those that address building codes, land use planning, and resource allocation.

3. To compare the seismic risk with other natural hazard risks.

The AEL figures, which include estimated losses in regions with infrequent earthquakes, can be compared with more frequent flood and wind-related losses. The ability to measure earthquake risk relative to other natural hazards helps in a balanced, multi-hazard approach to risk management. For example, elevating structures in response to flood hazard may compromise them in terms of earthquake risk and would suggest a different approach to risk reduction in that case.

2   Burby, Raymond and Peter May. Making Building Codes an Effective Tool for Earthquake Hazard Mitigation, Environmental Hazards, 1, 1999, p. 27-37.

3   Federal Emergency Management Agency, Report on the Costs and Benefits of Natural Hazard Mitigation, FEMA 294, 1997, Washington, D.C. U.S. Government Printing Office.

4. To support disaster response and recovery planning.

For planning for catastrophic earthquakes, the ability to compare annualized estimates of debris, casualties and shelter requirements on a regional, state and municipal scale enables planners to anticipate potential resource requirements under the National Response Plan. These estimates, along with the 250, 500 and 1000 year estimates, are useful in planning tools, as well as identifying and prioritizing mitigation measures that address life safety and functionality of essential facilities.

A Glossary

Annualized Earthquake Loss (AEL) – The estimated long-term value of earthquake losses in any given single year in a specified geographic area.

Annualized Earthquake Loss Ratio (AELR) – The ratio of the average annualized earthquake loss to the replacement value of the building inventory. This ratio is used as a measure of relative risk, since it considers replacement value, and can be directly compared across different geopolitical units including census tracts, counties, and states.

Average Annual Frequency – The long-term average number of events per year.

Basic Building Inventory – The national level building inventory incorporated into HAZUS-MH. The basic database classifies buildings by occupancy (residential, commercial, etc.) and by model building type (wall construction, roof construction, height, etc.). The basic mapping schemes are state-specific for single-family occupancy type and region-specific for all other occupancy types; they are building-age and height specific. The four inventory groups are: general building stock, essential and high potential loss facilities, transportation systems, and utilities.

Hazard – A source of potential danger or an adverse condition. For example, a hurricane occurrence is the source of high winds, rain, and coastal flooding, all of which can cause fatalities, injuries, property damage, infrastructure damage, interruption of business, or other types of harm or loss.

Hazard Identification – Hazard identification involves determining the physical characteristics of a particular hazard - magnitude, duration, frequency, probability, and extent – for a site or a community.

Hazards U.S. – Multi-Hazard (HAZUS-MH) – A standardized GIS-based loss estimation tool, developed by the Federal Emergency Management Agency (FEMA) in cooperation with the National Institute of Building Sciences (NIBS). See www.fema.gov/plan/prevent/hazus for more information.

Peak Ground Acceleration (PGA) – The maximum level of vertical or horizontal ground acceleration caused by an earthquake. PGA is commonly used as a reference for designing buildings to resist the earthquake movements expected in a particular location and is typically expressed as a percentage of the acceleration due to gravity (g).

Probabilistic Seismic Hazard Data – An earthquake ground motion estimate that includes information on seismicity, rates of fault motion, and the frequency of various magnitudes. Earthquake hazards are expressed as the probability of exceeding a level of ground motion in a specified period of time (e.g., 10% probability of exceeding 20% g in 50 years).
See http://earthquake.usgs.gov/ for more information.

Return Period – The average time between hurricanes of comparable size in a given location. Equal to the reciprocal of the frequency.

Risk – The likelihood of sustaining a loss from a hazard event defined in terms of expected probability and frequency, exposure, and consequences, such as, death and injury, financial costs of repair and rebuilding, and loss of use.

Risk Analysis – The process of measuring or quantifying risk. Risk analysis combines hazard identification and vulnerability assessment and answers three basic questions:

■ what hazard events can occur in the community?

■ what is the likelihood of these hazard events occurring?

■ what are the consequences if the hazard event occurs? The overall significance of these consequences in the community or region is called the risk assessment.

Risk Management – The reduction of risk to an acceptable level. Risk management addresses three issues:

- what steps should be taken to reduce risks to an acceptable level (mitigation),

- the relative trade-offs among multiple opportunities (benefit/ cost analyses, capital allocation), and

- the impacts of current decisions on future opportunities.

Spectral Acceleration (SA) – The acceleration response of a single degree- of-freedom mass-spring dashpot system with a given natural period (e.g., 0.3 of 1 second) to a given earthquake ground motion. SA is most closely related to structural response and, therefore, indicates an earthquake's damage potential.

Vulnerability Assessment – The process of assessing the vulnerability of people and the built environment to a given level of hazard. The quantification of impacts (i.e., loss estimation) for a hazard event is part of the vulnerability assessment.

B Overview of HAZUS

Acknowledging the need to develop a standardized approach to estimating losses from earthquakes and other hazards, FEMA has embarked on a multiyear program to develop a GIS-based regional loss estimation tool. FEMA released the first version of the HAZUS earthquake model in 1997 followed by an updated version in 1999. In 1998, FEMA began the development of a multi-hazard methodology to encompass wind and flood hazards.

FEMA developed HAZUS and HAZUS-MH under agreements with the National Institute of Building Sciences. HAZUS-MH is a tool that local, state, and federal government officials and others can use for mitigation, emergency preparedness, response and recovery planning, and disaster response operations. The methodology in HAZUS-MH is comprehensive. It incorporates state-of-the-art approaches for characterizing hazards; estimating damage and losses to buildings and lifelines; estimating casualties, displaced households, and shelter requirements; and estimating direct and indirect economic losses.

Since HAZUS-MH is a uniform national methodology, it serves as an excellent vehicle for assessing and comparing seismic risk across the United States. The HAZUS technology is built upon an integrated geographic information system (GIS) platform that produces regional profiles and estimates of earthquake losses. The methodology addresses the built environment, and categories of losses, in a comprehensive manner.

HAZUS-MH is composed of six major modules, which are interdependent. This modular approach allows different levels of analysis to be performed, ranging from estimates based on simplified models and default inventory data to more refined studies based on detailed engineering and geotechnical data for a specific study region.

A brief description of each of the six modules is presented below. Detailed technical descriptions of the modules can be found in the HAZUS technical manuals.[4]

---

4   Federal Emergency Management Agency, *HAZUS-MH MR2 Earthquake Model Technical Manual*, Prepared by the National Institute of Building Sciences for FEMA, 2006.

MODULE 1: POTENTIAL EARTH SCIENCE HAZARD (PESH)

The Potential Earth Science Hazard module estimates ground motion and ground failure (landslides, liquefaction, and surface fault rupture). Ground motion demands in terms of spectral acceleration (SA) and peak ground acceleration (PGA) are typically estimated based on the location, size and type of earthquake, and the local geology.

For ground failure, permanent ground deformation (PGD) and probability of occurrence are determined. GIS-based maps for other earth science hazards, such as tsunami and seiche inundation, can also be incorporated. In the current study, hazard data from the US Geological Survey is used.

MODULE 2: INVENTORY AND EXPOSURE DATA

Built into HAZUS is a national-level basic exposure database that allows a user to conduct a preliminary analysis without having to collect any additional local data. The general stock of buildings is classified by occupancy (residential, commercial, etc.) and by model building type (structural system, material and height). The default mapping schemes are state-specific for the single-family occupancy type and region-specific for all other occupancy types. They are age- and building-height specific.

The four inventory groups are: general building stock, essential and high potential loss facilities, transportation systems, and utilities. The infrastructure within the study region must be inventoried in accordance with the standardized classification tables used by the methodology. These groups are defined to address distinct inventory and modeling characteristics. A description of the model building types can be further examined in Chapter 3 of the HAZUS technical manual.

Population data is based on the 2000 United States Census[5] and estimates for building exposure are based on default values for building replacement costs (dollars per square foot) for each model building type and occupancy class, in addition to certain regional cost modifiers. Data also are drawn from Dun and Bradstreet and RS Means.

---

5   U.S. Bureau of the Census, "Standard Tape File 3," STF-3, 2002

MODULE 3: DIRECT DAMAGE

This module provides damage estimates for each of the four inventory groups based on the level of exposure and the vulnerability of structures (potential for damage at different ground shaking levels).

A technique using building fragility curves based on the inelastic building capacity and site-specific response spectra is used to describe the damage incurred in building components[6]. Since damage to nonstructural and structural components occurs differently, the methodology estimates both damage types separately. Nonstructural building components are grouped into drift-sensitive and acceleration-sensitive components.

For both essential facilities and general building stock, damage state probabilities are determined for each facility or structural class. Damage is expressed in terms of probabilities of occurrence of specific damage states, given a level of ground motion and ground failure. Five damage states are identified - none, slight, moderate, extensive and complete.

MODULE 4: INDUCED DAMAGE

Induced damage is defined as the secondary consequence of an event. This fourth module assesses dams and levees for inundation potential, and hazardous materials sites for release potential. Fire following an earthquake and accumulation of debris are also assessed.

MODULE 5: DIRECT LOSSES

Unlike many previous loss estimation methods, HAZUS-MH provides estimates for both economic and social losses. Economic losses include structural and non-structural building losses, costs of relocation, losses to business inventory, capital-related losses, income losses, and rental losses. Social losses are quantified in terms of casualties, displaced households, and short-term shelter needs. The output of the casualty module includes estimates for four levels of casualty severity at three daily time periods and for six occupancies and commuters. Casualties, caused by secondary effects such as heart attacks or injuries while rescuing trapped victims, are not included.

Shelter needs are estimated based on the number of structures that are uninhabitable, which in turn is evaluated by combining damage to the residential building stock with utility service outage relationships.

---

6   Kircher, C.A., et al., "Estimation of Earthquake Losses to Buildings," Earthquake Spectra, Vol. 13, No. 4, 1997, pp. 703-720.

MODULE 6: INDIRECT LOSSES

This module evaluates the long-term effects on the regional economy from earthquake losses. The outputs in this module include income and employment changes by industrial sector[7].

---

7   Brookshire, D.S., et al., Direct and Indirect Economic Losses from Earthquake Damage, Earthquake Spectra, Vol. 13, No. 4, 1997, pp. 683-702.

C Probabilistic Hazard Data Preparation and AEL Computation

The U.S. Geological Survey (USGS) provided the probabilistic seismic hazard data for the entire United States. A three-step process was used to convert the data into a HAZUS-compatible format.

STEP 1: COMPUTE THE PGA, SA@0.3 AND SA@1.0 AT EACH GRID POINT FOR THE EIGHT RETURN PERIODS.

The USGS provided the hazard data as a set of 18 (or 20) intensity probability pairs for each of the approximately 150,000 grid points used to cover the United States. For each grid point, a linear interpolation of the data was used to calculate the ground motion values corresponding to each of the eight return periods used in this study (100, 250, 500, 750, 1000, 1500, 2000, and 2500 years).

Table C-1 provides an example of the USGS hazard data for an individual grid point. In the table, for each of the 18 intensity-probability pairs, the intensity of the ground motion parameters (PGA, SA @ 0.3 sec. and SA @ 1.0 sec.) is shown along with the corresponding Annual Frequency of Exceedence (AFE). Step 2: Compute the PGA, SA@0.3 and SA@1.0 at each census tract centroid for the eight return periods.

For estimating losses to the building inventory, HAZUS uses the ground shaking values calculated at the centroid of the census tract. To incorporate the USGS data into HAZUS, the ground shaking values at the centroid were calculated from the grid-based data developed in Step 1.

Table C-1. Example of the USGS Hazard Data

#	PGA	AFE	SA (0.3 sec)	AFE	SA (1.0 sec)	AFE
			Ground Motion Data			
1	5.00E-03	2.49E-02	5.00E-03	3.28E-02	2.50E-03	2.85E-02
2	7.00E-03	2.07E-02	7.50E-03	2.89E-02	3.75E-03	2.37E-02
3	9.80E-03	1.65E-02	1.13E-02	2.40E-02	5.63E-03	1.84E-02
4	1.37E-02	1.25E-02	1.69E-02	1.85E-02	8.44E-03	1.34E-02
5	1.92E-02	8.76E-03	2.53E-02	1.30E-02	1.27E-02	9.24E-03
6	2.69E-02	5.86E-03	3.80E-02	8.45E-03	1.90E-02	6.25E-03
7	3.76E-02	3.87E-03	5.70E-02	5.29E-03	2.85E-02	4.23E-03
8	5.27E-02	2.64E-03	8.54E-02	3.36E-03	4.27E-02	2.95E-03
9	7.38E-02	1.90E-03	1.28E-01	2.27E-03	6.41E-02	2.14E-03
10	1.03E-01	1.43E-03	1.92E-01	1.63E-03	9.61E-02	1.60E-03
11	1.45E-01	1.08E-03	2.88E-01	1.19E-03	1.44E-01	1.18E-03
12	2.03E-01	7.73E-04	4.32E-01	8.28E-04	2.16E-01	8.08E-04
13	2.84E-01	5.06E-04	6.49E-01	5.03E-04	3.24E-01	4.83E-04
14	3.97E-01	2.88E-04	1.30E+00	1.30E-04	4.87E-01	2.36E-04
15	5.56E-01	1.35E-04	1.95E+00	3.84E-05	7.30E-01	9.04E-05
16	7.78E-01	4.88E-05	2.92E+00	7.62E-06	1.09E+00	2.60E-05
17	1.09E+00	1.32E-05	4.38E+00	9.76E-07	1.64E+00	5.08E-06
18	1.52E+00	2.80E-06	6.57E+00	8.61E-08	2.46E+00	6.62E-07

STEP 2: COMPUTE THE PGA, SA@0.3 AND SA@1.0 AT EACH CENSUS TRACT CENTROID FOR THE EIGHT RETURN PERIODS.

For estimating losses to the building inventory, HAZUS uses the ground shaking values calculated at the centroid of the census tract. To incorporate the USGS data into HAZUS, the ground shaking values at the centroid were calculated from the grid-based data developed in Step 1.

Two rules were used to calculate the census-tract-based ground shaking values:

1. For census tracts that contain one or more grid points, the average values of the points are assigned to the census tract.

2. For census tracts that do not contain any grid points, the average value of the four nearest grid points is assigned to the census tract. Using this method, census-tract-based ground motion maps are generated for all eight return periods.

STEP 3: MODIFY THE PGA, SA@0.3 AND SA@1.0 AT EACH CENSUS TRACT CENTROID TO REPRESENT SITE-SOIL CONDITIONS FOR A NEHRP SOIL CLASS TYPE D.

The USGS data were based on a National Earthquake Hazard Reduction Program (NEHRP) soil class type B/C (medium rock/very dense soil). For this study, NEHRP soil class type D (stiff soil) was assumed for all analyses. To account for the difference in soil class types, the data developed in Step 2 were modified. The procedure described in Chapter 4 of the HAZUS technical manual was used for the modification of the ground shaking values.

AVERAGE ANNUALIZED EARTHQUAKE LOSS COMPUTATION

After the hazard data was processed, an internal analysis module in HAZUS transformed the losses from all eight scenarios into an Annualized Earthquake Loss (AEL).

The calculation of AEL is illustrated in Table C-2A. HAZUS computes Annual Losses for eight probabilistic return periods as shown in the Return Period column. The Annual Probability of the occurrence of the event is 1/RP. The Differential Probabilities is obtained by subtracting the Annual Occurrence Probabilities. Next the Average Loss is computed by averaging the Annual Losses associated to various return periods as shown in the column Average Losses. Once average loss is computed, the Average Annualized Loss is the summation of the product of the Average Loss and Differential Probability of experiencing this loss. Table C-2B shows a sample computation for Average Annualized Loss.

Figure C-1 illustrates schematically a HAZUS example of eight loss-numbers plotted against the exceedence probabilities for the ground motions used to calculate these losses.

HAZUS computes the AEL by estimating the area under the loss probability curve as represented in Figure C-1. This area represents an approximation to the AEL and is equivalent to taking the summation of the differential probabilities multiplied by the average loss for the corresponding increment of probability. In effect, one is approximating the area under the curve by summing the area of horizontal rectangular slices.

The choice for the number of return periods was important for evaluating average annual losses, so that a representative curve could be connected through the points and the area under the probabilistic loss curve be a good approximation. The constraint on the upper bound of the number was computational efficiency vs. improved marginal accuracy. To determine the appropriate number of return periods, a sensitivity study was completed that compared the stability of the AEL results to the number of return periods for 10 metropolitan regions using 5, 8, 12, 15 and 20 return periods. The difference in the AEL results using eight, 12, 15 and 20 return periods was negligible.

Table C-2A and B Average Annualized Earthquake Loss Computation

#	Return Period	Annual Probabilities	Differential Probabilities		Annual Losses	Average Losses	Annualized Loss
			Formula	Values			
1	2500	0.00040	P2500	0.00040	L2500	L2500	P2500 x L2500
2	2000	0.00050	P2000 - P2500	0.00010	L2000	(L2500+L2000)/2	(P2000 - P2500) x (L2500+L2000)/2
3	1500	0.00067	P1500 - P2000	0.00017	L1500	(L2000+L1500)/2	(P1500 - P2000) x (L2000+L1500)/2
4	1000	0.00100	P1000 - P1500	0.00033	L1000	(L1500+L1000)/2	(P1000 - P1500) x (L1500+L1000)/2
5	750	0.00133	P750 - P1000	0.00033	L750	(L750+L1000)/2	(P750 - P1000) x (L750+L1000)/2
6	500	0.00200	P500 - P750	0.00067	L500	(L750+L500)/2	(P500 - P550) x (L750+L500)/2
7	250	0.00400	P250 - P500	0.00200	L250	(L250+L500)/2	(P250 - P500) x (L250+L500)/2
8	100	0.01000	P100 - P250	0.00600	L100	(L100+L250)/2	(P100 - P250) x (L100+L250)/2
							$\Sigma(\quad)$

#	Return Period	Annual Probabilities	Differential Probabilities	Annual Losses	Average Losses (Billions of $)	Annualized Loss (Billions of $)
1	2500	0.00040	0.00040	5.700	5.700	0.00228
2	2000	0.00050	0.00010	5.290	5.495	0.00055
3	1500	0.00067	0.00017	4.660	4.975	0.00083
4	1000	0.00100	0.00033	3.020	3.840	0.00128
5	750	0.00133	0.00033	2.600	2.810	0.00094
6	500	0.00200	0.00067	1.900	2.250	0.00150
7	250	0.00400	0.00200	1.020	1.460	0.00292
8	100	0.01000	0.00600	0.425	0.723	0.00434
						0.01463

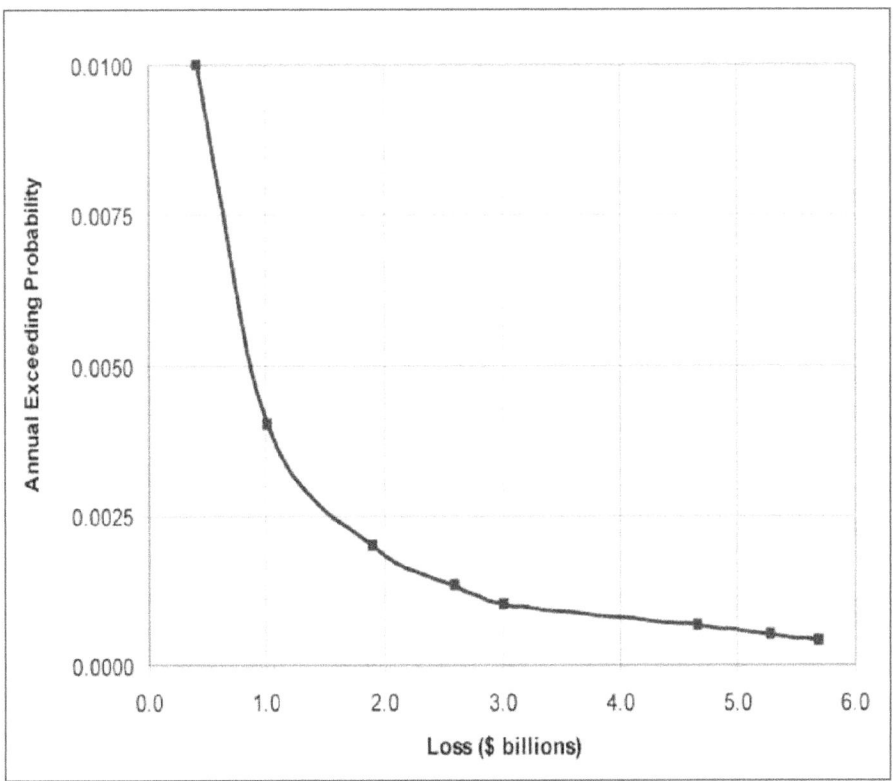

Figure C-1.
Probabilistic Loss
Curve